Coffee:
Too Hot to Handle
or
Mishandled?

A Guide to the Prevention of
Hot Beverage Spills & Burn Lawsuits

Coffee:
Too Hot to Handle
or
Mishandled?

A Guide to the Prevention of
Hot Beverage Spills & Burn Lawsuits

DAN COX

*with Technical Editor and
Contributing Author, Spencer Turer*

ONION
RIVER
PRESS

191 Bank Street
Burlington, Vermont USA

Coffee: Too Hot to Handle or Mishandled?
A Guide to Preventing Hot Beverage Spills and Burn Lawsuits

Copyright 2019 by Dan Cox

Technical editor and contributing author, Spencer Turer
Photographs by Julia Luckett
Cover and book design by Lindsay Francescutti

ISBN: 978-1-949066-07-4
LCCN: 2018948338

Publisher's Cataloging-in-Publication data

Names: Cox, Dan C., author. July 13, 1949
Title: Coffee: too hot to handle or mishandled? a guide to hot beverage spills and burn lawsuits / by Dan Cox.
Description: Includes bibliographical references. | Burlington, VT: Onion River Press, 2018.
Subjects: LCSH Products liability--Food--United States. | Liability (Law)--United States. | Food law and legislation--United States. | Coffee Industry--United States. | Personal injuries--United States. | BISAC LAW / Liability | BUSINESS & ECONOMICS / Industries / Food Industry
Classification: LCC KF1297.F6 C69 2018 | DDC 614.3--dc23

Published by Onion River Press
191 Bank Street
Burlington, VT 05401

Table of Contents

Preface vii

Introduction xi

Chapter 1: Brewed & Sued
Hot Beverage Spill Litigation 1

Chapter 2: Spill Prevention
Cups, Lids, Warnings, and Handling..49

Chapter 3: Matters of Degree
Brewing Temperatures and Scald Burns....................................89

Chapter 4: Best Practices
Recommendations for Commercial Operations..........................121

Afterword..173

Acknowledgments 177

Appendix 179

Contributors...183

Preface

The coffee industry is a rich and diverse community of people and businesses. Over the course of my career, I have been privileged to participate in several professional capacities. I am currently the owner of Coffee Enterprises, an independent consulting firm with coffee and tea laboratories. My work allows me to keep abreast of industry issues and changes with regard to coffee quality, brewing and serving equipment, product innovations, and consumer safety.

As the landscape of the hot beverage industry has flourished and grown, spills and burn lawsuits have developed too. I became interested in this issue in 1999 when retained in a lawsuit as an expert witness on industry brewing standards and the temperatures required to brew hot coffee. To date, I have been called to serve in that role in more than forty cases. And, from what I now see, there are half a dozen or more hot coffee, hot tea, or hot chocolate lawsuits in progress at any given time. Most are settled out of court—but not all.

What have we and what haven't we learned in the decades that followed the infamous 1994 hot coffee spill and burn lawsuit, *Liebeck v. McDonald's* (a product liability case that became the flashpoint for seemingly frivolous lawsuits)? Why are we still "taking the stand" to talk about the required brewing temperatures for hot coffee and tea when the facts regarding such are scientific, substantiated, and proven? Why do hot drink spills persist, and why is there any need for this second book?

This is what I know: the problem does not lie with hot beverage brewing temperatures. The problem arises from the fact that coffee-drinking habits in North America have changed. In other places and cultures, such as Italy, a shot of espresso is served in a small cup and quickly consumed while seated in cafés or standing at coffee bars. In Turkey, making and serving coffee is part of a rich cultural heritage and is meticulously prepared and brewed twice before it is poured into tiny cups. In Japan, you can find both hot and cold coffee served in cans from vending machines. In Ethiopia, the birthplace of coffee, the preparation and serving of coffee are a ceremonious event that takes hours. Decades ago, most people in the United States sat down in restaurants, offices, or at kitchen tables to drink their hot beverages from six- or eight-ounce ceramic cups with handles and saucers. They rarely spilled, and to the best of my knowledge, they never sued.

Times have changed. The good news is that more and better coffees and teas are readily available in cities and small towns nationwide. The worrisome news is that the hot drinks are not handled with enough care. Much of the time, if consumers are seated, they are seated in moving vehicles and are drinking the hot beverages on the go. In the US, millions of cups of hot coffee and tea are made, purchased, and served every day in paper or Styrofoam cups to-go. Twelve, sixteen, and twenty-ounce cups are lidded and unlidded, sugar added, cream poured, drive-thru windows navigated, and takeout trays precariously balanced. Harried baristas and flight attendants juggle taking orders, payments, and pouring drinks. Consumers rush and maneuver hot drinks while driving, walking, jogging, flying—and do so with briefcases, laptops, phones, steering wheels, shopping bags, or young children and baby strollers in hand. Fortunately, most of the time, the only result of such multi-tasking is that busy consumers have enjoyed a pleasant pick-me-up and warming hot drink. Sometimes there are minor upsets such as when a besieged barista hands out regular instead of decaffeinated or adds whole milk instead of skim. But on other more rare and unfortunate occasions, people spill hot drinks. Sometimes those spills are large enough to result in significant scald burns. And sometimes the injured patrons sue their coffee purveyors.

So, what should we do? Turn back the clock and ask people to slow down, stop, sit, and then sip? Lower the brewing temperatures and serve insipid, flavorless drinks? Clearly, we enjoy flavorful hot beverages as well as the convenience of drinking them on the go. The solution does not lie with turning back time or tampering with proper brewing temperatures and ruining flavor profiles. The answer is in solving how to handle to-go hot beverages more safely. My first book, *Handling Hot Coffee,* focused on the scientific justification for the high temperatures necessary to brew flavorful hot coffee and tea. This second book, *Coffee: Too Hot to Handle or Mishandled?* adds to that work by reviewing more lawsuits to uncover the most common causes of hot drink spills. It also offers specific, practical suggestions to increase consumer safety and reduce hot beverage spills and lawsuits.

Ideally, I hope that the millions of daily hot coffee and tea drinking customers neither spill their drinks nor are burned. And I hope that no company is sued… however, if that does happen, may this guide prove to be a supportive professional resource. May it also help generate impetus for the hot beverage industry to lead the way in spill prevention.

Dan Cox
Founder and President of Coffee Enterprises
Past President of the Specialty Coffee Association of American
Co-founder of Grounds for Health
Recipient of the Specialty Coffee Association of America's "Man of the Year" and Distinguished Service Award
Recipient of the Lifetime Achievement Award from the Specialty Coffee Association of America
Past Chairman Coffee Quality Institute

Coffee Enterprises **Coffee Analysts** **Tea Analysts** **Dan Cox & Associates** **Grounds for Health**

Introduction

This book is intended as a comprehensive reference for the coffee and hot beverage industry—its foodservice operators and its lawyers. It provides scientific and evidential validation of temperature standards in the context of hot beverage litigation and serves to help retail establishments prepare a successful defense if sued. Until the 2013 publication of my first book, *Handling Hot Coffee*, the industry lacked a single resource in which the pertinent, diverse subjects were compiled—food science, spill prevention, warnings, thermal scald burn information, and litigation.

In addition to providing the scientific information that substantiates necessary brewing temperatures for coffees and teas, *Coffee: Too Hot to Handle or Mishandled?* reviews the common causes of hot beverage spills and offers the foodservice industry informed, practical suggestions to avoid spills and litigation. The first chapter reviews many hot beverage lawsuits and the causes common in spills, claims in litigation, and examines research about how people attribute blame. The second chapter looks at spill prevention and the role of cups, lids, hazard warnings and compliance. It also addresses specific concerns and considerations for hot drink service at drive-thrus and on airlines. The third chapter looks at beverage temperatures, the burn severity equation, and scald burns—including why the mouth does not burn with a sip, but a spill can cause serious burns. It also reviews studies of consumer temperature preferences and the expected serving temperatures of hot beverages. (It is worth noting, for example, that manufacturers have raised the internally-set brewing temperatures of consumer coffee-brewing equipment to that of commercial operations.)

Lastly, the book includes a comprehensive section of best practice recommendations for commercial operations—brewing, holding, safe handling of hot beverages, and what to do after a spill.

Coffee: Too Hot to Handle or Mishandled? strives to provide pertinent, research-based information and suggestions that will prove helpful in keeping consumers safe and foodservice operators off the hotplate as we work to keep pace with the industry's enormous growth. Today's hot drink retail environment is jam-packed with opportunities for sales in almost any venue: traditional coffee shops, fast service outlets, convenience stores, gas stations, supermarkets, kiosks, carts, stadiums, airport and train terminals, etc. We are a mobile culture with "to-go" expectations. We drink beverages while we drive. We have created drive-through lanes and expect delivery from establishment-to-vehicle to be convenient and speedy. We drink unlidded cups of hot drinks, precariously placed, while buckled into seats on crowded airplanes. Cup holders are now standard in cars, trucks, motorcycles, shopping carts, and baby strollers.

It is not enough that we are taking hot beverages with us wherever we go. We multitask as we drink. We've added cell phones and other electronic devices into the mix—talking and texting, watching the navigation screen, checking the internet—while driving two tons of steel with one hand on the wheel, one hand holding a beverage or phone, and one eye on the road. We are running out of hands and eyes! This does not seem like the ideal environment to drink hot tea or coffee—and is not the way it was originally intended to be consumed. How do we adapt and proceed safely?

In the midst of this hectic, demanding, consumer-driven retail environment, the hot beverage industry weighs its consumers' product expectations and preferences with the product's hazard risks. This is a challenging equation to balance, particularly when the necessary temperatures involved in creating and maintaining a quality product usually pose little or no risk when consumed as intended—with full sensory focus and slow, exploratory sips. Yet when a quantity of any hot liquid—coffee, tea, cocoa, water, or soup—lands on someone's body it can cause life-altering burns.

So what is the solution? In terms of costs, a company can spend only so much on consumer spilled hot beverage litigation before it feels a compulsion to fight back. Yet by doing so, a company risks harming its business image and future sales; companies cannot afford to ignore public perception of misconduct. Remember the infamous 1994 *Liebeck vs. McDonald's* case? The $2 million-plus that Mrs. Liebeck was initially awarded seemed outrageous. Even when the punitive damages were reduced to $480,000 upon appeal, the amount appeared excessive. Are we crazy? She spilled coffee on herself and admitted it! No matter how you feel about tort reform, that case became a tipping point and lesson in business image and responsiveness. The court found in favor of Mrs. Liebeck stating that the company knew there was a problem, ignored consumer safety, and displayed "willful, wanton, and reckless behavior." For the hot beverage industry, the Liebeck case illustrates the importance of approaching burn incidents from both a beverage-quality and a legal perspective. In this case, McDonald's was within industry standards for beverage temperature; however, its handling of the incident was viewed as callous, unsympathetic, and the company appeared to accuse Mrs. Liebeck of wrongdoing on the stand.

Has the industry been responsible and held accountable? Yes and no. Have consumers? Yes and no. But now it is time for everyone to wake up, smell the coffee, and do better at preventing spills and burns.

A good starting place to discover workable solutions is to look at how other safety hazards are handled. In terms of food and beverage safety, existing standards have been primarily concerned with allergy cautions and the microbiological hazards of food safety and the sanitation of handler environments. Restaurant restrooms have mandatory signs requiring employees to wash their hands before handling food or serving customers. Many restaurants, following

US Food and Drug Administration guidelines, have placed a warning statement in small print at the bottom of their menus, such as "Consuming raw or undercooked meats, poultry, seafood, shellfish, or eggs may increase your risk of foodborne illness." Now the food and beverage safety concerns must go beyond temperature and microbiological hazards and consider the burn risks from accidental spills.

What are effective and practical risk management and safety solutions? Stakeholders in the hot beverage industry must join ranks to set safety standards for its products and raise public awareness about handling hot drinks with more caution. Manufacturing innovations in safer cup and lid designs must be tested to standards, affordable to produce, and purchased by the industry. Foodservice operators must diligently warn consumers of the inherent burn risk hot beverage spills impose and urge them to handle hot drinks with more care.

Employers must also create an internal culture of safety. Employee training is crucial. It is essential that employers educate staff regarding the spill risks when handling hot beverages and implement protocols and safety measures to avoid spill accidents and burns. It is important to distinguish between what is considered an acceptable, reasonable risk and what circumstances increase that risk to become unnecessarily dangerous, such as serving unprepared, unlidded hot drinks to travelers, or using poor-quality cups with insecure lids.

As has been seen in court, consumer behaviors often compound hot drink spill and burn risks significantly. For example, although a thermal scald burn can result in serious injury, the lawsuit still can be found frivolous—even if second- or third-degree burns were sustained. If people were fooling around while holding cups of hot coffee, any resulting lawsuit would be considered frivolous. If you stirred cream and sugar into an unlidded cup of hot coffee while in a moving vehicle and it spilled onto your lap causing second- or third-degree burns, it would likely be considered an unfortunate incident, but a lawsuit without merit. Many of the lawsuits found in Chapter One demonstrate that suffering even serious burns would not necessarily result in the assignment of blame to purveyors. When consumers spill hot liquids in their own homes and are burned, a lawsuit almost never occurs; however, when hot liquids are purchased in a commercial establishment, many consumers file claims for damages—even when they were not careful and spilled it on themselves.

Ideally, we will reach a point when judges, juries, and consumers alike will understand that high temperatures are necessary to achieve consumer-acceptable, flavorful, hot coffees and teas. We will also appreciate and use due caution when handling hot beverages. We would see fewer lawsuits, fewer spills, and fewer burns. I hope that this book will move us closer toward that goal.

CHAPTER ONE

Brewed & Sued
Hot Beverage Spill Litigation

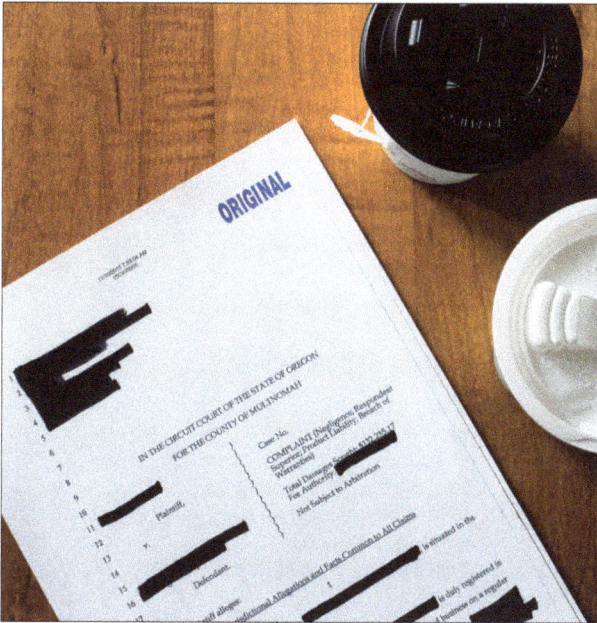

The coffee business is booming—some would describe it as trendy and hot. Crowds of eagerly caffeinated and decaffeinated customers sip their favorite hot beverages while multi-tasking and hustling through busy days. We drink hot coffee and tea in cafés and restaurants, while traveling in cars, jostled on subways or buses, cramped and constrained on airplanes, running errands, and on the way to our offices and homes. But enjoying our hot drinks while rushing to and fro has rendered us cavalier and careless. Unwary actions have contributed to countless spills, serious burns, and "brewed and sued" litigation.

We know and expect that when we order coffee, tea, or cocoa from a café, it will be served hot—just like pizza from steel or brick ovens, french fries from deep fryers, and soup from the kitchen pot. We are accustomed to blowing on the surface of hot tea, coffee, cocoa, or soup before taking a sip; we allow fries or cheese pizza to cool slightly before taking a bite. Despite our common knowledge that these foods and drinks are served hot, we are nevertheless surprised to find that when a cup of hot soup, coffee, tea, or cocoa spills on our skin, it can cause considerably more damage than just redness or minor blisters that heal within days. Why would the heat of familiar hot beverages render us such a surprise? Has our safe and frequent consumption reduced our caution and vigilance? What has made a hot beverage spill repeatedly more likely to result in litigation than a tumble of french fries or pizza? Are hot beverage temperatures higher than other foods?

Pizza ovens are typically set above 450°F (232.2°C), and some restaurants with wood-fired or brick ovens are set at over 700°F (371.1°C). Thus, pizza fresh from the oven will be hot enough (particularly with the oils and more viscous hot cheese), to burn human skin. Soup is cooked to boiling 212°F (100°C) or held at simmering of about 195°F (90.5°C) before serving in a foodservice establishment. French fries are cooked by immersing sliced potatoes in hot oil between 325°and 375°F (162.7-190.5°C). Coffee is brewed at temperatures between 195° and 205°F (90.5-96.1°C). And our exposed human skin is vulnerable; it burns with just a thirty-second exposure at 130°F (54.4°C).

When pizza with hot cheese burns, its likely burn site is your mouth, lips, or tongue—you drink a glass of water and relief immediately begins; or, when a startled or clumsy move causes a pizza spill, the slice probably drops to the table or floor. But when a quantity of hot tea, coffee, cocoa, or soup spills on a person's body, it can saturate clothing quickly and burn through layers of skin.

More than two decades of hot beverage spill litigation have provided plaintiff testimonies as evidence that demonstrate it is not common knowledge for consumers to recognize a hot beverage spill can quickly cause skin burns damaging enough to require medical treatment and hospitalization. Stunned by the severity their injuries, consumers often claim that the beverage must have been excessively hot and therefore defective under the law to cause such significant injury.

That belief is mistaken. It is not so; as with many other common hot foods, the requisite temperatures to properly prepare the items—in this case, to brew, hold, and serve hot coffee, cocoa, or tea—are well above skin burn thresholds. Further, people's routine behaviors demonstrate that they are familiar with and do have a good sense of the temperature range of their everyday hot beverages—most people take a few small exploratory sips, blow across the surface, and drink when the beverage reaches their preferred temperature. I have been called in as consultant or expert witness in forty-plus cases of hot beverage spill incidents resulting in litigation—and not one has involved burns to the mouth or tongue while sipping or drinking.

Whether made at home or purchased at a restaurant, most good quality commercial and home coffee makers brew at ranges between 195-205°F (90-96.1°C), the temperatures needed to extract necessary aroma and taste compounds from ground beans. A May 15, 2018 article in *Consumer Reports* (CR), "Fastest Coffee Makers From CR's Tests," affirms these temperatures as the "sweet spot" for quality home coffee makers: "For drip coffee makers, we conduct a brew-performance test to measure the brew temperature and contact time (how long water stays within the sweet spot of 195°F to 205°F for brewing)." Hot tea, cocoa, or manually prepared pour-over coffees are usually made with hot water just off the boil and a little under 212°F (100°C).

These temperatures are not new, excessive, or out of the ordinary. We have enjoyed sipping hot coffee served at similar temperatures around the world for six centuries. Hot coffee and tea are safe when handled as intended—sipped in small quantities by mouth—a common occurrence when both customers and companies act with befitting caution and reasonable care.

Adding condiments to a hot beverage while
seated in a vehicle is never a good idea!

Today, however, there are many ways we unwittingly compound the inherent dangers from a hot beverage spill; a considerable number of spills take place while someone was driving, riding, walking, or fiddling with the lids to add dairy products or sweeteners. Spills in a moving vehicle are particularly hazardous. Drivers and passengers often encounter the unexpected—abrupt stops, sharp turns, potholes, or air turbulence in a plane—and avoiding a hot beverage spill may be hindered by seatbelts, fellow passengers, or crowded conditions.

Nevertheless, much of the focus in hot beverage spill and burn litigation has been on the temperature of the drink, as well as a failure to warn that hot coffee and hot tea are served hot enough to burn if spilled and require careful handling. The fact that hot beverage spills can cause serious burns is not proof that a beverage was served excessively hot or is a defective product. The past two-plus decades of spill litigation (with its focus on brewing temperatures), has diverted our attention from a more thorough investigation of the underlying cause(s) of hot beverage spills and unheeded consumer warnings. Today, we welcome the development and implementation of practical, effective, spill-preventing solutions.

What follows are several examples of hot beverage spill lawsuits. Patterns emerge and underlying issues are revealed when multiple incidents are examined and compared. It is hoped that this chapter will offer the hot beverage industry—including foodservice operators, airlines, hoteliers, hospitals, as well as cup and lid manufacturers—the galvanizing information and impetus needed to tackle hot beverage spill prevention with confidence.

Frivolous and Not-so Frivolous Lawsuits

Perhaps the most famous—and misunderstood—coffee spill litigation was the 1994 jury trial of *Liebeck v. McDonald's Restaurants, P.T.S., Inc.*[1] It created a nationwide media stir and became fodder for columnists and comedy show ridicule when a jury initially awarded Mrs. Liebeck more than two million dollars in punitive damages for injuries she suffered after admittedly spilling hot coffee on herself.

While parked in the McDonald's parking lot and seated in the passenger seat, Mrs. Liebeck put a cup of hot coffee between her legs (there was no cup holder) and attempted to remove the lid on the cup to add cream and sugar. The coffee spilled onto her lap. She was scalded and suffered second- and third-degree burns on her thighs, buttocks, and groin area requiring hospitalization and skin grafts. Third-degree burns are devastating injuries that penetrate the skin down to the subcutaneous fat, muscle, and bone. She was permanently disfigured and was partially disabled for almost two years. Mrs. Liebeck acknowledged that she spilled the coffee on herself, but she testified that she expected only minor and uncomfortable burns, and not the serious third-degree burns, pain, and suffering she sustained.

Initially, Mrs. Liebeck did not sue, but wrote to McDonald's and asked for two things: one, that the company check for defects and reevaluate the temperatures at which they brewed and served coffee, and two, she asked them to cover medical expenses and lost income related to her injuries. McDonald's refused her request for changes in policy and offered $800. Mrs. Liebeck then retained legal counsel and filed a civil lawsuit alleging that the coffee was defective because it was excessively hot and adequate warnings were not provided regarding the burn risks of coffee at that temperature.

McDonald's did not argue whether its hot coffee could cause serious scald burns; in fact, the company made their coffee well within accepted industry-wide recommendations: brewed at

195-205°F (90.5-96.1°C) and served between 180-190°F (82.2-87.7°C). However, in testimony, a safety consultant for McDonald's stated that the company had received over 700 prior coffee burn complaints over the previous ten years and that the number of complaints was considered statistically insignificant when compared to the millions of cups McDonald's served over a year.

Once the jurors saw the severity of Mrs. Liebeck's burns, heard the evidence, and deliberated, they returned a verdict in her favor on the claims of product defect, breach of implied warranty of merchantability, and breach of implied warranty of fitness for a particular purpose. They also found Mrs. Liebeck to be twenty percent at fault. The court stated that the corporation knew there was a problem and ignored consumer safety. The judge declared that McDonald's displayed "willful, wanton, and reckless behavior." The jury awarded Mrs. Liebeck $200,000 in compensatory damages, reduced the award by $40,000 (Liebeck's twenty-percent fault), for a net compensatory judgment of $160,000. In addition, for McDonald's "reckless" conduct, the jury awarded Mrs. Liebeck punitive damages that were the equivalent of two days of

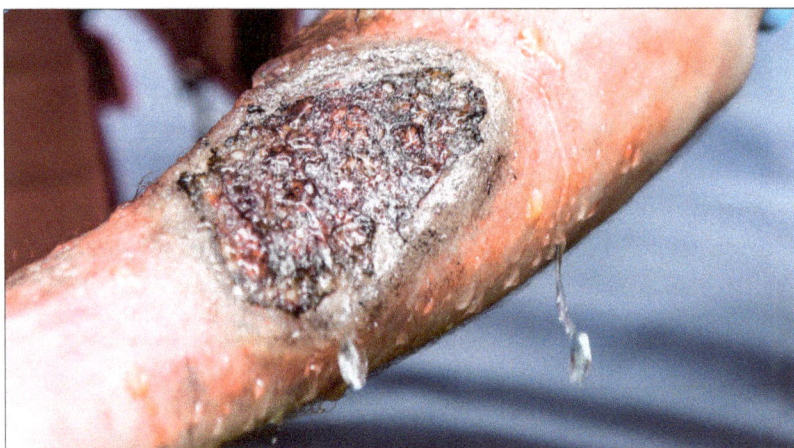

Here is an image of a third-degree thermal scald burn such as was suffered by the plaintiff in the infamous 1994 lawsuit, *Liebeck v. McDonald's Restaurants, P.T.S., Inc.*

McDonald's coffee sales revenue—the widely reported 2.7 million dollars—which was later reduced by the trial judge to the much less well-publicized amount of $480,000. Mrs. Liebeck appealed, the appeal was denied, and the judge ordered a post-appeal conference at which the parties agreed to settle for an undisclosed and confidential amount.

Widely and wrongly reported as having awarded millions of dollars, the public decried the *Liebeck v. McDonald's* case as a frivolous lawsuit with a "jackpot jury." The presumptive popular lore about Mrs. Liebeck is that an older woman was burned when she blundered and spilled her hot coffee, refused to accept personal responsibility, and was awarded outlandish sums of money by a foolhardy jury. It made for simple, compelling headlines, but that tale was not an accurate, informed, or unbiased story. The real object lesson from *Liebeck v. MacDonald's* is that burns from hot coffee spills should be taken as seriously as the damage they can cause—neither consumers nor retailers can afford to be lax when handling hot beverages. The harm that can result is neither insignificant nor frivolous.

Seventeen years after *Liebeck v. McDonald's*, Susan Saladoff, a former attorney, directed the documentary *Hot Coffee*,[2] which presents the facts of the Liebeck case in rebuttal to the "common knowledge" that it was a frivolous lawsuit. Based on the evidence submitted, the court had correctly determined that the Liebeck suit was not frivolous. A frivolous act is one without substance or merit; in legal terms, it refers to a lawsuit or motions within that suit that are "intended to harass, delay, or embarrass the opposition" and "lacks any [legal] basis."[3] In *Hot Coffee*, Saladoff interviewed people she encountered on the street about the Liebeck case and contrasted the assumptions they had from media coverage of the case with their reactions to the severity of the injury after viewing photographs of Mrs. Liebeck's burns. Her interviewees expressed common surprise that a coffee spill could cause such severe debilitating burns—not to overlook the accompanying personal and financial harm.

Saladoff uses the *Liebeck* case and other cases to highlight the negative side of tort reform—laws that limit the type or amount of damages that may be awarded in personal injury lawsuits—and its infringements on an individual's right to sue and seek compensation through legal action. Although this book is concerned with the distinction between frivolous and legitimate lawsuits, it is not meant as a commentary on tort reform.

One research study was fashioned using the *Liebeck v. McDonald's* lawsuit as a model: "How do People Attribute Blame for Burns Sustained from Hot Coffee? The Causal Attributions,"[4] by Michael J. Kalsher, Gregory M. Phoenix, Michael S. Wogalter, and Curt C. Braun. In this study, eighty-four participants were presented with systematically varied information related to a fictitious product liability case (loosely based on a set of scenarios from *Liebeck v. McDonald's*), to "examine how people assign blame for injuries sustained during the use of or exposure to consumer products." The participants included twenty-eight undergraduates from a private technical university and fifty-six non-student volunteers from the local community. (Forty-four males, mean age 30.6 years, and thirty-six females, mean age 38.4, and four participants did not provide gender information.) Forty-two percent of the participants reported having had minor burns from hot coffee prior to the study and fifty-eight percent had not. Nearly all said they had some degree of familiarity with the *Liebeck v. McDonald's* coffee case.

The study's introduction stated the following:

> Safety researchers have begun to systematically examine how people view responsibility for safety. Of particular interest is how people assign blame for injuries sustained with use of consumer products. Perceived responsibility is an important concern in

the area for several reasons. If a product manufacturer assumes that consumers are responsible for their own safety, for example, then safety-related concerns may not be incorporated into the design of the product and the accompanying instructions or marketing efforts intended to promote it. If, on the other hand, consumers view the manufacturer to be responsible for the safety of the product, they may not be careful while using the product. Given either scenario, safety may be compromised, and personal injury and/or property damage might occur. Perceptions of responsibility are also an important consideration, given the increasingly litigious society in which we live. Thus, knowing how jurors form perceptions concerning who is responsible for product safety will be of interest to persons involved in product liability cases.

The study included evaluation of participants' product familiarity (McDonald's hot coffee) as well as their general perception of hot coffee spill hazards. It found "On average, respondents reported a low likelihood of being injured by McDonald's coffee, but indicated that one must be moderately careful when drinking it. Fifty-five percent of respondents reported that the product was 'safe and very unlikely to lead to /cause personal injury,' while forty-one percent indicated that the product posed 'a hazard that could result in minor personal injury.' Only three percent of the participants indicated that the product posed 'a hazard that could result in severe personal injury.'" These results are noteworthy given that most participants expressed prior knowledge of and familiarity with the *Liebeck v. McDonald's* case, but they were far less familiar with the severity and degree of Mrs. Liebeck's burns.

Accompanying many hot beverage lawsuits' allegations that the product was defective because it was excessively hot are claims that there was a failure to warn of burn hazard dangers. The study's participants also evaluated hot beverage product warnings: "After viewing the coffee cup warning label, respondents indicated that the warning was moderately noticeable, but that people would only be somewhat likely to read it. Participants also indicated that the warning would only be somewhat effective in getting people to be more cautious when they handle the cup as it is served. When asked to define the term 'Hot' in degrees, the average reported temperature was 166.7° Fahrenheit."

This study's findings are particularly relevant: only three percent of participants in the sample study believed that spilling hot coffee on themselves could result in severe personal injury. From this worrying insight, the researchers deduced that "participants' relatively low perceptions of the danger associated with this product (hot coffee) and the actual potential for injury (at 180-185°F/82.2-85°C) [typical holding and serving temperature] suggests the presence of a 'hidden hazard.'" They also suggest further study of improved warnings with stronger signal words, such as "Extremely Hot." They conclude, "Finally, there is a need for research to systematically investigate how defendants might be viewed if they were to take *steps to decrease the likelihood and extent of injury, such as changes to the design of the container (e.g., to the cup and lid), more effective warnings, or better employee training practices.* Such changes might impact people's causal attributions, and in turn, alter the way in which they allocate responsibility for consumer product injuries."

We believe that this study suggests a call to action. It offers industry leaders an opportunity to raise the bar, not in court, but in consumer awareness, risk management, and spill prevention. Foodservice operators, product designers, and cup and lid manufacturers must join forces to develop and use products that prevent or reduce spills and increase consumer safety. Specific suggestions for cup and lid safety, warnings, best practices, and staff training will be discussed in detail in chapters 2 and 4 of this book.

Common Claims
Product liability, design defect, negligence, failure to warn

Courts of law and government agencies have induced many industries to improve consumer safety and protection from products with unforeseen dangers or hidden hazards. Dramatic safety risks such as those found in the automotive industry compelled car manufacturers to develop innovations such as seatbelts, airbags, safety glass, and collapsible steering wheels. Over-the-counter pharmaceutical companies added tamper-proof safety caps and pamphlets with detailed usage and side-effect warnings. These advances proved to reduce or prevent injuries and save lives. But a manufacturer or seller need not incorporate unconditional safety features into its product so that no harm will come to a user—no matter how careless he or she may be. Products are not required to be accident-proof and failsafe under any and all conditions. It cannot be done with cars, and it cannot be done with hot beverages. Society and the legal system expect that consumers will use reasonable caution with products that have inherent, obvious dangers. Would a retailer be expected to sell a dull knife because it was safer to touch?

As unfortunate and serious as a scald burn can be, injury alone does not establish that the hot beverage at issue was excessively hot or exceeded acceptable temperatures. When a quantity of any hot liquid—tap water, cooking oil, cocoa, coffee, soup, or tea—spills on the skin, a third-degree burn can occur in as little as five seconds at 140°F (60°C); notably, temperatures at which hot coffee or tea would not be considered a properly made or served product. Nonetheless, some plaintiffs and their expert witnesses have argued that hot tea and coffee should be made and served at significantly lower temperatures to prevent serious burns. However, if brewed at temperatures low enough to remove the risk of burns, coffee and tea would no longer have their signature tastes or aromas. They would be insipid flavors in tepid waters.

One common statement and admission in hot beverage spill lawsuits is that although consumers knew and expected their coffee, tea, or cocoa to be served hot, they were not aware of the serious burns that could result from a spill of their cup of afternoon tea or morning joe. This lack of awareness regarding the hazard of serious scald burns when hot beverages are spilled accounts for many plaintiffs' allegations that the beverage was served excessively hot in product liability and design defect claims. Defendants counter that argument with evidence that heat was inherent to the quality of a good cup of coffee or tea. Judges often agree that it is reasonable and common knowledge for the average consumer to know that hot beverages pose obvious burn risks because the dangerous aspect is inherent to the quality of the product (as analogous to the type of obvious danger posed by a sharp knife). Plaintiffs' familiarity with hot drinks and acknowledgment that hot beverages could cause burns have been used as evidence in court proceedings to support defendants' assertions that the inherent burn risk is foreseen and common knowledge.

Nonetheless, plaintiffs often counter they were exposed to harm "to an extent beyond that contemplated by the ordinary consumer," and therefore, there was negligence or a failure to warn. Although it often does appear true that many consumers do not yet comprehend how dangerous a spill from their home-brewed or purchased hot beverage can be, that lack of awareness does not make it true that the beverage served was excessively hot.

Courts have traditionally used the consumer expectations test and the reasonable care balancing test to evaluate plaintiffs' product liability and design defect claims. To pass the consumer expectations test, plaintiffs must present evidence that the coffee was hotter than normal and more than would be expected by the reasonable consumer; to pass the reasonable care balancing test defendants

Cups that are not securely placed in cup holders
could spill scalding hot liquid on tender skin.

must present evidence that the temperature was appropriate and that the heat an essential element of a quality cup of coffee, tea, or another hot beverage.

A third possible legal test is a risk-utility analysis. This test asks whether the risk of using the product is outweighed by the utility of its design and whether a reasonable alternative design existed. This test does allow the fact-finder to consider consumer expectations, although those consumer expectations do not determine whether a product is defective, and the plaintiff may be expected to show reasonable alternative designs.

In failure to warn claims, plaintiffs contend that the hot beverage was defective because adequate warnings did not accompany the cup to inform consumers that severe burns could result from a spill. Plaintiffs must also offer evidence that the alleged inadequacy of the warning caused the injuries. For plaintiffs to claim successfully that the failure of an adequate warning caused the incident, they need to show that they would have acted differently had they been provided with the hypothetical warning. Defendants often assert they did not have a duty to warn because the danger of burns [from coffee or tea] is open and obvious.

It is worth considering: What other hot foods come with such warnings? A bowl of chicken noodle soup or pot of cheese fondue? Eggs and fish are considered to have inherent hidden hazards, and most restaurant menus do warn, but should supermarkets warn too?

Are hot beverage hazards open and obvious? Or, are the dangers posed by spilling hot beverages hidden hazards unforeseen by reasonable consumers? And if that is the case, then wouldn't adequate warnings be a prudent course for all foodservice operators and good risk managers?

Case Examples

Numerous restaurant owners and operators, airlines, and convenience store owners have been taken to task and court over hot beverage spills and consumers' burns. The case examples that follow strive to illustrate the common claims in hot beverage spill and burn litigation as well as bring attention to legal strategies and contrasting court decisions.

In 1998, just a few years after the *Liebeck v. McDonald's* lawsuit made headlines, another hot coffee spill caused second-degree burn injuries, the plaintiffs filed similar claims (the coffee was excessively hot, and there was a failure to warn), but there was a notably different legal decision: *Holowaty v. McDonald's Corp.*[5] Here are some of the pertinent excerpts from the court reports:

> On July 9, 1995, the plaintiffs [Mr. and Mrs. Holowaty] were traveling through Rochester, Minnesota when they stopped at a McDonald's

restaurant for breakfast. Mr. Holowaty purchased food, juice, and a large cup of coffee. A McDonald's employee placed the drinks in a beverage tray and gave them to Mr. Holowaty. The coffee was in a Styrofoam cup covered by a lid. The cup and lid contained warnings that stated 'HOT!' and 'CAUTION: CONTENTS HOT.'

Before leaving the restaurant, Mr. Holowaty removed the lift-tab on the lid of the coffee cup, creating an opening in the drink. Plaintiffs then carried the beverage tray and food items to their car. When they reached the vehicle, Mrs. Holowaty sat in the passenger seat with the beverage tray on her lap.

Plaintiffs drove down a steep decline when they exited the parking lot. As they traveled down the slope, the coffee tipped and spilled about half its contents onto Mrs. Holowaty. The coffee soaked into Mrs. Holowaty's shorts and caused second-degree burns to her upper and inner thighs. The burns took two months to heal, and Mrs. Holowaty has permanent scars.

The Holowatys filed suit against McRick Inc., the franchise owner of the McDonald's restaurant, as well as McDonald's, the franchisor. The Holowatys' lawsuit alleged design defect, failure to warn, negligence and breach of warranty. Their claim contended that the coffee was defective because it was excessively hot and that McDonald's did not provide adequate warnings about the severity of the burns that could result from a spill.

To help support their design defect claim based on their presumption that the coffee served was excessively hot, the Holowaty's called upon Dr. Kenneth Diller, a professor of biomedical and mechanical engineering to testify as an expert witness.

Diller's report stated that "the risk of a thermal burn associated with serving coffee at temperatures in the range of 180 [degrees] to 190 [degrees] Fahrenheit is unacceptable." From the perspective of lowering the probability of thermal burns from hot beverage spills, Diller commented that "150 [degrees] is a much safer temperature for serving beverages, and leading burn experts have recommended a temperature of 135 [degrees] or lower."

McDonald's countered there was no design defect because the coffee was not excessively hot as heat is an inherent quality of coffee and it was not hotter than regularly served; therefore, it was not defective. McDonald's presented expert testimony from Ted Lingle, a coffee brewing specialist and one of the founders and executive directors of Specialty Coffee Association of America. According to Lingle:

> The temperatures employed to 'brew' and 'hold' coffee are an exact science....Unless water is heated to the proper temperature the flavor will not be extracted from the coffee grounds. The optimal temperature for brewing coffee is between 195 and 205 degrees Fahrenheit. The coffee industry recommends brewing coffee within this temperature range, and brewing temperatures between 195 and 205 [degrees Fahrenheit] are standard in commercial coffee equipment...Coffee should be held at a temperature between 175 and 185 degrees for maximum flavor. The standard holding temperature in the industry is within the same temperature range.

The courts then used the reasonable care balancing test and the consumer expectations test to evaluate the Holowatys' claim that the coffee served was defective.

To prevail under the reasonable care balancing test, the Holowatys would have needed to show that the coffee they purchased was unreasonably dangerous because it was hotter than it should have been, or, that a reasonable restaurant owner would have sold coffee at a lower temperature. They were unable to do so. The court responded to the Holowatys' expert witness testimony stating that "Diller does not have expertise in coffee brewing and cannot offer any opinion about the possibility of brewing and holding coffee at the temperatures he recommends," and Diller also did not put forward that any restaurant owner would have selected a different brewing or holding temperature for the coffee.

McDonald's, however, did provide evidence that its brewing and holding temperatures were within industry recommendations for commercial coffee sales, and in fact, evidence in the record indicated that the manager of this McDonald's franchise set the temperature slightly lower than average in a commercial setting—at 190°F and 180°F (87.7 and 82.2°C) for brewing and holding, respectively.

Under the consumer expectations test, a food product is considered defective if the harm-causing characteristic of the product would not have been expected by a reasonable consumer. The Holowatys were unable to provide evidence that the coffee was hotter than normal. Thus, the design defect claim failed under both tests. Further, because the Holowatys were not able to show that the product was defective and "not fit for the ordinary purpose for which such goods are sold," the court decided there was no breach under the implied warranty of merchantability. A product is not defective when it is safe for normal handling and consumption.

The Holowatys also claimed that McDonald's had a duty to warn because "the risk of injury was more severe than a reasonable consumer would anticipate." The Holowatys admitted that they knew the coffee would be hot and could cause burns. However, they argued that they also thought spilled coffee would only cause reddened skin, and therefore, reasonable consumers anticipate only minor burns and do not know that the coffee can produce second-degree burns. Thus, they argued McDonald's had a duty to warn because the public is not aware of the severe burn hazard.

McDonald's contended they did not have a duty to warn because the danger of burns from hot coffee spills is open and obvious; secondly, McDonald's stated there was insufficient proof that the alleged inadequacy of the warning caused Mrs. Holowaty's injuries.

The duty to warn claim was rejected by the court because "the type of injury the average consumer would anticipate and the injury that resulted were different in degree, not in kind." In other words, the spectrum of injury possible (from a first- to a third-degree burn) does not change the fundamental nature of the injury (a burn, as opposed to a cut or an illness).

McDonald's motion for summary judgment was granted, and the Holowatys' complaints were dismissed with prejudice as the facts were undisputed, and the law was clear there were no grounds to proceed to a trial. The court decided there was no design defect, no failure to warn, no negligence, and no implied warranty of merchantability. Of further interest, under the causation and failure to warn claim, the court stated, "Plaintiffs admit they were aware that the coffee was hot, and that it could cause burns if spilled. Plaintiffs also knowingly took the coffee into a moving vehicle, compounding the danger. A reasonable person taking hot coffee into a car would handle the coffee with care. Thus, even if Defendants had included a warning that stated 'DANGER: COFFEE CAN CAUSE SEVERE BURNS' there is no reason to believe that Plaintiffs would have altered their conduct."

The next three examples further illustrate court perspectives when evaluating hot beverage product liability cases. Again, readers will note that despite the degree and seriousness of plaintiffs' injuries, the fact that an injury occurred does not suffice as evidence that a product was unreasonably dangerous or defective. Product liability claims must be presented in court with objective evidence that the product is defective in its design, manufacturing, or marketing.[6] In sum, the degree of injury does not center on the presumption that a product is unreasonably dangerous solely because an injury occurred.

Here is one example from a 2010 hot beverage spill lawsuit, *Colbert v. Sonic Restaurants, Inc.*[7]:

On February 7, 2008, Gerald Colbert ("Colbert") drove to the Sonic Restaurant in Mansfield, Louisiana to purchase a cup of coffee from the restaurant drive-thru. Colbert made a special request to the order taker at Sonic that Sonic add cream and artificial sweetener when preparing his coffee. However, on that date, the Sonic employee handed Colbert his cup of coffee along with the cream and artificial sweetener to put in his coffee instead of adding it to his coffee before bringing it to him, as he had requested. After receiving his coffee, Colbert pulled forward, placed his car in park, and removed his foot from the brake. While sitting in his car, Colbert placed his coffee on the console. After doing so, and while holding his cup of coffee with his right hand, Colbert used his left hand to remove the lid so that he could add the cream and sweetener. With his left hand, he took off the lid. The hot coffee splashed on his right hand and caused an instantaneous reaction causing the coffee to be spilled into his lap. He sustained second-degree burns through his blue jeans in his groin area, stomach/abdomen area and thigh.

Colbert asserts that prior to February 7, 2008, whenever he purchased coffee from a restaurant, including Sonic, he would make a special request that the restaurant add cream and artificial sweetener when preparing his coffee and that restaurants, including Sonic, usually honored his request.

Colbert filed suit in state court against Sonic and its insurer, alleging that Sonic was negligent and failed to warn him and other customers of hot coffee, failed to keep its coffee at a proper temperature and failed to make sure its coffee cups were in a safe condition. Colbert further alleged that Sonic 'knew or should have known that the cup was overfilled with hot coffee and should have warned plaintiff and other customers of hot coffee cups' and that Sonic's coffee was unreasonably dangerous.'

The court granted the restaurant and the insurer's motions for summary judgment and all claims made by the customer against the restaurant and the insurer were dismissed. Why?

First, the court found that Mr. Colbert had not met his burden of proof regarding his claim that the coffee temperature was excessively hot. Colbert submitted an affidavit in which he tried to support his claim that the coffee was unreasonably dangerous by stating that "upon the Sonic cup of coffee spilling over him, he saw steam rising from the coffee and going through his car window as if the steam was rising from boiling water." Therefore, Colbert asserted that the coffee was at least 212°F (100°C) based on the rising steam and his knowledge from high school chemistry class that water boils and turns to steam at that temperature. He also submitted hearsay of other customers' statements that "the coffee is too hot" or they "must wait for it to cool before drinking," to try to further support his claim.

In this case, I was called upon to testify for the defense as coffee expert and expert witness. In my deposition, I testified that

This driver has his hands full and defines dangerous driving while distracted—a steering wheel, a cell phone, and a hot drink in a tilted cup.

although I did not know the temperature of Colbert's coffee on the day of his burn, I was able to confirm the industry's recommended brewing temperature for hot coffee is 200 degrees, plus or minus five degrees, and the holding temperature is 185-190 degrees. Additionally, I attested to the likelihood that Sonic's coffee machine brewed at the industry suggested temperatures because other than routine cleaning, brewing equipment manufacturers do not recommend allowing on-site operators the ability to make adjustments to their equipment.

I was then cross-examined by Colbert's counsel about how the temperature of Sonic's coffee is regulated:

> Q: And I can tell you that you've told me that you don't know the temperature of the coffee that—on

that day Gerald Colbert was burned at Sonic. Now my question is, if you don't know the temperature of the coffee that day that Gerald Colbert was burned, how can you candidly tell me and the court that the coffee was within the industry standards temperature-wise?

A: The way brewing equipment is configured today is that there are upper and lower thermostats on the equipment…if the temperature of the liquid coming out of the machine is too low, there is a thermostat which will not allow the machine to brew; and if the temperature is too hot, it will not allow this machine to brew. Since neither of those were indicated I can say with the probability that the machine was within the brewing temperatures, but as to whether—the exact temperature on that day—I cannot say.

Colbert also claimed that there was inadequate hazard warning. But again, the law maintains that a manufacturer's duty to warn does not extend to dangers that are or should be obvious or common knowledge to the ordinary user or handler of the product. Vendors only have a duty to warn consumers about the temperature of a beverage if it exceeds industry standards or was hotter than normal.

Colbert failed to provide the evidence necessary to meet his burden of proof that the product he was served was defective and exceeded industry standards. Colbert also acknowledged that he was a frequent coffee drinker, had purchased coffee from Sonic numerous times before the incident, continued to purchase coffee from the vendor after the accident, and had spilled coffee on himself previously. Due to his experience and common sense knowledge, the court believed that Colbert should have known of the dangers inherent in drinking hot coffee, as well as of the compounding risk associated with opening the lid of a hot cup of coffee while in an automobile. The restaurant's motion for summary judgment was granted, and all claims made by the customer were dismissed with prejudice.

This unlidded cup of hot tea may be more than 200°F (93.3°C).
Human skin burns in just one second at 156°F (68.8°C).

The second example is a hot tea spill and burn lawsuit from 2015. Hot tea is often made to order at or near boiling temperatures and served immediately. If spilled, hot tea can cause very serious burns, as occurred in a California case: *Graham v. Yum Yum Donut Shop, Inc.*[8]

In this incident, the plaintiff, Ms. Graham, purchased a large hot tea and a bag of donuts. She specifically asked for the cup to be left unlidded. She walked next door and back to her place of employment where she then placed the cup of hot tea and the ribbon-tied bag on the counter. Graham picked up the bag and struggled to untie the knotted bow, her hand slipped, knocked the cup of hot tea over, and the hot contents spilled onto her chest. She suffered third-degree burns, required hospitalization, plastic surgery, and was permanently scarred. Graham claimed the tea was served excessively hot. She was offered a settlement but refused it, and the case went to a jury trial. Again, the defendants called upon me as their expert witness to verify standards for brewing hot teas and coffee, and despite Graham's significant injuries, the jury returned their verdict with a 12-0 count in favor of the defendant. Graham received no compensation for her unfortunate injuries or reimbursement for medical expenses.

The third example involves an incident where an airline passenger suffered serious second- and third-degree burns from a hot coffee spill: *Lamkin v. Braniff Airlines, Inc.*[9]

In March of 1985, a married couple was on a Braniff flight from Miami to Boston. Shortly after take-off, a flight attendant served hot coffee to Helen Lamkin. The court reports the incident and proceedings as follows:

> Mrs. Lamkin put the coffee on a folding shelf attached to the seat in front of her. The passenger seated in front of her moved the seat backward, which caused the coffee cup on the folding shelf to spill its contents onto Mrs. Lamkin's lap. Mrs.

Lamkin sustained what was later diagnosed as second- and third-degree burns from the coffee. She went to the bathroom to attend to the burns. The flight crew had no ice packs to apply to the burns, but Mr. Lamkin applied ice, apparently from the aircraft's galley, to the burned area.

On the day following the incident, a defective coffeemaker was removed from the plane on which Mrs. Lamkin was injured. The evidence does not reveal the precise defect in the coffeemaker except that a note on a Braniff services form states that 'there was no power to brew.'

Mrs. Lamkin filed suit against Braniff claiming negligence in hiring, instructing, and training of its flight personnel in serving hot coffee and providing first aid, as well as Braniff's use of an allegedly defective coffeemaker, seats, cup, and folding shelves. She also claimed that Braniff was negligent in failing to warn her about the excessively high temperature of the coffee, and in failing to warn the passengers about the hazards of moving a seat back.

The plaintiffs offered one expert, Stephen Capitoline [sic], an aviation safety expert. He testified at deposition that he had no opinion as to whether the seat tray was defective; that he had no information on which to base an opinion that Braniff's procedures or training for in-flight services were negligent; that he knew nothing about proper or safe temperatures for coffee on airplanes; and that he knew nothing about the proper and safe functioning of an airplane's coffeemaker.

The court granted the airline's motion for summary judgment and concluded that the plaintiffs had not shown enough evidence to support a finding by a factfinder that Braniff was negligent:

> The plaintiffs have failed to offer any evidence that Braniff knew or should have known that there was a defect in the coffeemaker which would cause it to brew extremely hot coffee. Indeed, the plaintiffs have not even shown that there was a defect in the coffee-maker that caused it to brew extremely hot coffee. The plaintiffs have not offered any evidence to show that Braniff or any of its employees knew or should have known that the coffee which was actually served to Mrs. Lamkin was extremely hot. In short, the plaintiffs have simply failed to offer any evidence which would support a finding of negligence.
>
> The plaintiffs cannot prevail on their failure to warn claim because Mrs. Lamkin was aware that the coffee was hot.... Moreover, the plaintiffs have not shown that any Braniff employees were aware that the coffee was hot enough to burn Mrs. Lamkin; i.e., that any Braniff employees knew or should have known that there was anything unusual about which Mrs. Lamkin should have been warned.
>
> In addition, the plaintiffs have not offered any evidence to suggest that the flight attendants on her flight acted negligently with respect to Mrs. Lamkin's care after the coffee spilled. The plaintiffs have also failed to show how any behavior of the flight attendants after the coffee spilled exacerbated her injury. Finally, the plaintiffs have not offered any evidence as to how the seats, seat trays or cups were defective.

Airlines may serve hot drinks to first-class passengers in unlidded
porcelain cups, but first-class luxury is still a first-class danger.
Hot beverages served without lids or secure cup holders
can spill easily—with or without turbulence.

Because the court decided that the plaintiff failed to provide
sufficient evidence to allow a jury to conclude that the airline
acted negligently, the airline's motion for summary judgment was
granted. There was no negligence shown, no failure to warn, and
the doctrine of *res ipsa loquitor* (a doctrine whereby in certain,
limited circumstances negligence is presumed from the accident at
issue) was not applicable.

In this regard, the court commented:

> Neither the plaintiffs' expert nor common
> knowledge supports a finding that the mere
> occurrence of this accident shows negligence.,

Mr. Chapdelaine [sic], the expert offered by the plaintiff, by self-acknowledgment is not qualified to testify as to the cause of the accident. He has no particular expertise regarding the proper functioning and maintenance of a coffee machine. As noted above, he admitted that he has no specialized knowledge which would permit him to render an opinion on the proper temperature at which coffee should be served on an airplane. Nor does Mr. Chapdelaine [sic] have any expertise regarding the procedure for in-flight service.

Moreover, the Court is not persuaded that a jury may reasonably infer negligence from their general knowledge of practical affairs merely because a passenger is burned by hot coffee. A jury would have no way of knowing whether the coffee served to the plaintiff was hotter than coffee customarily served on airplanes or in places of public accommodation. Thus, a conclusion that the brewing of extremely hot coffee was due to negligence would be based on speculation and guesswork.

Courtroom Evidence & Expert Witnesses

It is essential for plaintiffs and defendants to present specific, verifiable evidence. In many lawsuits, as illustrated above, plaintiffs and/or defendants rely upon the testimony of expert witnesses to strengthen their cases—with notably mixed results. A good expert witness is by definition well-qualified with pertinent expertise. It is someone who "by reasons of education or special training, possesses knowledge of some particular subject area in greater depth than the public at large."[13] Expert witnesses are brought into court to provide objective, professional opinions based on facts pertinent to the case at hand—a good expert witness is not called to voice personal opinions nor to be an advocate for either side.

The Daubert standard is the test used by a trial judge in federal courts and in many state courts "to make a preliminary assessment of whether an expert's scientific testimony is based on reasoning or methodology that is scientifically valid and can properly be applied to the facts at issue. Under this standard, the factors that may be considered in determining whether the methodology is valid are: (1) whether the theory or technique in question can be and has been tested; (2) whether it has been subjected to peer review and publication; (3) its known or potential error rate; (4) the existence and maintenance of standards controlling its operation; and (5) whether it has attracted widespread acceptance within a relevant scientific community."[10]

The lawsuits discussed above offer lessons for attorneys defending similar cases and demonstrate the importance of choosing an appropriately qualified expert witness as part of a strong litigation strategy. For example, in the Liebeck case, McDonald's attorneys were not well prepared with the appropriate expert(s) to defend the new legal theory and strategy of "defective due to temperature." Further, McDonald's lawyers did not challenge the plaintiff's expert witness who was a professor of biomedical and mechanical engineering and an authority in heat and temperature related processes in living tissues and its application in the design of therapeutic devices. As bright and capable as that expert was, he was not an industry expert in the brewing and steeping temperatures required for the proper extraction of flavor from coffee beans or tea leaves, or the proper functioning and maintenance of brewing equipment.

By contrast, the defendants in the Holowaty, Colbert, and Lamkin lawsuits were well prepared with industry experts qualified to testify about temperatures required and equipment used for brewing hot coffee. The plaintiffs' expert witnesses were not qualified or able to demonstrate that the beverages were defective due to excessively high temperatures. Holowaty relied upon the professor of biomedical and mechanical engineering; Colbert relied on self-assessment from a high school chemistry class and customer hearsay; Lamkin called upon an aviation safety expert who admitted that he had he had no specialized knowledge that would permit him to render an opinion on the proper temperature at which coffee should be served on an airline. Courts render decisions based upon verifiable facts and not, as the *Lamkin v. Braniff* judge ruled, "...speculation and guesswork."

As can be seen in several of the lawsuits described above, a plaintiff's presumption and unsubstantiated claim that a hot beverage was defective and excessively hot because they suffered a burn does not often hold up in court—nor do many allegations that the hazard from a hot beverage spill was hidden, and the company failed to warn adequately. Frequently, the courts have decided that no warning was needed because plaintiffs were clearly familiar with the normal serving temperatures of the hot beverage and were therefore knowledgeable and held accountable. It is unfortunate that consumers' familiarity with serving and drinking temperatures have not yet, nor often, translated to their awareness that hot beverage spills can quickly cause serious burns.

If, however, the court did find there were reasonable prevention options available to the hot beverage provider at the time of the spill, which were known or should have been known but were ignored, the tables could turn. In that situation, the defendant could face substantial punitive damages for negligence. The hot drink purveyor would then see a two-dollar beverage turn into punitive damages and a not-so-frivolous lawsuit, such as occurred in *Liebeck v. McDonald's*, or more recently, *Mogavero v. Starbucks*.[11]

In *Mogavero v. Starbucks* (May 2017), a Duval County, Florida court ordered Starbucks to compensate Joanne Mogavero more than $100,000 for medical bills, pain, and suffering. She was severely burned and scarred after a lid popped off her cup at a Jacksonville restaurant's drive-thru. In this incident, Ms. Mogavero stated that she accepted a 20-ounce "venti" cup of hot coffee, and as she prepared to hand it to her passenger, the lid popped off and hot coffee spilled onto her mid-section and lap. Ms. Mogavero suffered first- and second-degree burns and was left with permanent scarring. She premised her claim of negligence and failure to warn alleging that the employee either did not place the lid on the cup securely or the lid was defective and not adequately inspected, and, that Starbucks should warn its customers of the lid's tendency to pop off. During testimony, a Starbucks representative stated that the company receives about 80 complaints a month about lid leaks and lids popping off and argued that it "would not be relevant" to warn customers of the risk. However, the jury did not concur and assigned 80 percent of the incident's negligence to Starbucks Corporation, 20 percent to Joanne Mogavero, and awarded her a little more than $15,492[14] for medical bills, as well as $85,000 for pain and suffering, physical impairment, disfigurement, inconvenience, and loss of capacity for enjoyment of life.

In another Florida Starbucks incident in 2015, a customer pulled his car up to the drive-thru window and ordered two breakfast sandwiches along with two large cups of coffee. Reportedly, the Starbucks' employee took payment and delivered a bag with just the food. The employee then returned to the window holding the first of the two coffees. With one cup of coffee in hand, the employee reached out of the store window toward the customer's hand and confirmed that he had securely gripped the coffee cup before letting it go. The customer placed the coffee in his vehicle's cup holder, and then the Starbucks' employee reached out to hand him the second cup of coffee. This time, however, the customer alleged that the employee released the cup before confirming it was safely placed into his hand, and the cup's contents spilled onto his lap. Immediately burned and in pain, the driver quickly exited his car and then jumped back in to drive home and tend to his burns. Once at home, he saw that his skin was peeling away from his groin and thighs, whereupon his friend drove him directly to the local hospital's emergency department. After his examination and emergency care, he was transferred via ambulance to a medical burn center where it was found that he suffered second-degree burns to his groin and thigh area and needed follow-up care with a plastic surgeon.

The customer sought legal counsel, filed a formal complaint, and the case was settled out of court. The plaintiff claimed that Starbucks breached its duty and was negligent by failing to properly transfer the cup, by serving coffee heated to a temperature that was dangerous and unfit for human consumption, and by failing to warn of such dangers. The specific complaints asserted that Starbucks breached its duty by failing to take the following actions:

a. Failing to train its staff as to how to transfer cups of scalding hot coffee at the drive-thru window;

b. Failing to have an appropriate system in place to transfer cups of scalding hot coffee at the drive-thru window;

c. Failing to properly transfer the coffee to Plaintiff;

d. Failing to provide coffee at a reasonable temperature so as to not burn its business invitee patrons;

e. Failing to warn, or adequately warn, Plaintiff that the coffee it served was heated to a temperature that was dangerous and would cause second-degree burns;

f. Providing coffee to Plaintiff that was heated to a temperature that made it unsafe for handling and/or consumption by humans.

The transfer and "hand-off" of hot beverages to car drivers and passengers at drive-thru windows is precarious for both servers and

A child strapped into a car seat with a hot cocoa is always a bad idea—
even if the cup is lidded. One bump or slippery turn and the contents
could spill scalding hot liquid on tender skin.

customers to execute safely. The height and angles of drive-thru
windows and different model vehicles are not consistent or well
aligned. When you compound this risk factor with the removal of
lids, adding and stirring condiments, cramped quarters without
stable flat surfaces—inside a moving vehicle—you have created a
good recipe for spills and second- or third-degree burn disasters.

Hot coffee is not the only beverage on the proverbial hotplate
and adults are not the only ones who spill and are burned. Hot tea
and hot cocoa are often served to children whose small hands and

everyday behaviors can readily lead to spills and burns requiring hospitalization, surgical treatments such as skin grafts, and permanent disfigurement. In just the last twenty-four months, I have been consulted in several cases where children have been seriously burned: in New York, a child was sliding across the back seat of the car with a cup of hot tea in hand, the child became caught up in a

seatbelt, spilled the tea, and suffered second- and third-degree burns; in Iowa, a child at a hospital cafeteria knocked over an unlidded cup of tea made from a self-serve hot water dispenser and suffered second- and third-degree burns to the sternum area; in California, a child grabbed a hot coffee from a hotel's continental breakfast table, spilled it, and suffered second-degree burns. What follows are the details of another incident involving a child and a hot cocoa spill. This case was litigated and brought to trial:

A 2002 Kansas jury trial involved an eleven-year-old boy, Kristopher McCroy, and his mother, Marie McCroy. (*McCroy ex rel. McCroy v. Coastal Mart, Inc*[12]). Ms. McCroy purchased a hot chocolate at a Coastal Mart convenience store (from a self-service foodservice commercial cappuccino machine manufactured by Wilbur Curtis, Co.), for her son to drink while riding home in the back seat of their conversion van. Before leaving the store, Kristopher placed a lid on the cup and inserted a straw. As his mother waited to leave Coastal Mart's parking lot, the child lifted the straw out and touched it to his tongue to test the temperature of the drink. He then tested a second time. A drop of hot cocoa spilled on his hand, caused him to flinch and release the cup. The cup overturned, the lid came off, and the hot cocoa spilled onto his lap. He suffered first- and second-degree burns. The McCroy allegations were that the hot chocolate's excessive temperature rendered it unreasonably dangerous, and therefore, the product was defective. The McCroys also asserted that more prominent and detailed warnings were needed to adequately warn of the specific injuries that could result.

Expert witness for the defense and coffee industry expert Ted Lingle stated in deposition testimony that according to industry standards, hot liquids, including soups, teas, and coffees are generally served at temperatures between 160 and 180°F. Courtroom testing of the machine in question repeatedly dispensed product well within that range.

In this case, the jury awarded Kristopher McCroy damages of $75,000 but also held all four principals accountable: his mother, Ms. McCroy was deemed 50 percent responsible for the accident; Kristopher 20 percent; Wilbur Curtis (the machine's manufacturer), 20 percent; and Coastal Mart was assigned 10 percent.

Hot beverage spill dangers exist whether in hospital cafeterias, hotel lobbies, restaurants, homes, or in cars. But these cases, and others, have led to my firm conviction that young children should never be given hot drinks when passengers in moving vehicles— not ever.

The following section contains a shortlist and abbreviated view of several other hot beverage spill and burn incidents—some of which were litigated and others were settled out of court.

Moltner v. Starbucks Coffee Co.[13]

CIRCUMSTANCES: The plaintiff, Ms. Moltner, purchased a "venti" sized cup of tea at a Starbucks cafe. Her tea was served double-cupped and lidded. She took it back to a table and tried to remove the lid to add sugar but had difficulty removing the lid. In her attempts to pry it off, the tea spilled onto her leg and foot

This is an extremely dangerous way to hold or transfer a hot beverage.
Lids may not be secure nor able to support the weight of a filled cup.
Never hold a cup from the top!

causing first and second-degree burns severe enough to require a skin graft and hospitalization.

CLAIMS: Plaintiff alleged product liability, defective design, and negligence. She claimed that Starbucks prepared tea with water that was too hot, that double cupping and placing a lid on the inner cup was defective design, and there was a failure to warn that the tea could overflow and spill when the lid was removed.

OUTCOME: The court determined that the fact that a cup of liquid may spill when the lid is removed is entirely within the realm of common knowledge and calls for no special warning.

I was the expert witness for the defense and confirmed the appropriate brewing temperatures for the beverage. The testimony of the plaintiff's expert witness was deemed inadmissible because it was judged "unreliable and devoid of factual or analytical grounds" for its summary opinions and conclusions. The district court's grant of summary judgment for the defendant was upheld on appeal, and the plaintiff's claims were dismissed.

Wurtzel v. Starbucks Coffee Co.[14]

CIRCUMSTANCES: The plaintiff, Ms. Wurtzel, requested a hot and an iced coffee to-go from inside a Starbucks café. She walked back to her car with the coffees and placed the hot coffee into the car's cup holder and the iced coffee on the passenger seat. She drove away, and as she was making a right-hand turn, the hot coffee spilled onto the back of her left leg, right thigh, and buttock. She suffered second-degree burns and scarring. She alleged that Starbucks failed to properly secure the lid to her coffee cup.

CLAIMS: Plaintiff claimed negligence based on the allegation that the Starbucks' employee failed to properly place the plastic lid on the cup securely.

OUTCOME: The court that determined the turning of the car without the circumstance of a loose lid was sufficient to have caused the cup's contents to spill. The testimony of the plaintiff's expert witness was considered inadmissible because his (lid) experiments were notably dissimilar from the facts of the case as to be irrelevant. Defendant's motion for summary judgment was granted on a claim of negligence, and the *res ipsa loquitor* theory of liability was ruled inapplicable.

McMahon v. Bunn-O-Matic Corp.[15]

CIRCUMSTANCES: The plaintiffs, Mr. and Ms. McMahon, stopped while on a trip and bought a cup of coffee from a mini-mart Mobil station. Upon their return to the car, Mrs. McMahon removed the hot coffee's plastic lid and began to pour a portion of the coffee into another smaller cup for Mr. McMahon so that it would be "easier for him to handle as he drove." As she attempted to do this, the hot coffee flooded her lap. She suffered second- and third-degree burns and was incapacitated for four months. She had permanent scars on her left thigh and lower abdomen. The plaintiffs believe that the Styrofoam cup collapsed either because it was poorly made or because the "inordinately hot coffee" weakened its structure.

CLAIMS: The plaintiffs filed lawsuits against Bunn and the manufacturers of the Styrofoam cup and plastic lid: product liability, duty to warn, and design defect. Plaintiffs claimed Bunn's coffee-making machine was defective and unreasonably dangerous because it made coffee at an extremely high temperature and Bunn breached a duty to warn consumers about the dangers of its hot coffee.

OUTCOME: Claims against the producers of the cup and lid were settled but their claims against Bunn remained. Defendants' motion for summary judgment was upheld on appeal regarding both product defect and failure to warn claims. The court decided there was no duty to warn because there was not sufficient evidence the coffee served was unusually hot or dangerous, and, consumers general product knowledge and experience made a warning unnecessary. Further, the court held there was no evidence of a design defect because the opinions of the plaintiff's expert witness were not based on facts or data.

Nadel v. Burger King Corp.[16]

CIRCUMSTANCES: Plaintiff-appellant Paul Nadel was driving and passengers in the car were his mother, his two daughters, and his son. The son was seated in the middle front seat between the plaintiff and his mother. They stopped at the drive-thru window of a Burger King and ordered sandwiches, drinks, and two cups of hot coffee. The plaintiff received and then handed a cardboard carryout tray with the two cups of lidded coffee to his mother. Plaintiff began to drive away and make a left turn onto the street. His mother was placing or had placed the containers down when his son started screaming. Plaintiff claims that the cups tipped, and the coffee spilled onto the child's right foot. He suffered second-degree burns.

CLAIMS: Breach of warranty of merchantability, breach of warranty of fitness for a particular purpose, product liability for a defective product, and failure to warn. The plaintiffs alleged that (1) the coffee was excessively hot and therefore defective, and (2) the defendants breached a duty to warn consumers about the dangers inherent in handling extremely hot coffee.

OUTCOME: The court held that there was no intervening super-seding cause. Summary judgment for defendant was granted regarding claims for breach of warranty of merchantability and fitness for particular purpose, as well as for claims of negligence toward business invitees and negligent infliction of emotional distress. Summary judgment for defendant was not granted with regard to claims of design defect and failure to warn. Summary judgment for defendant also was not granted on the question of punitive damages.

Note: A subsequent hot beverage spill and burn lawsuit, *Bouher v. Aramark Servs., Inc.,*[17] overruled Nadel and held that summary judgment for the defendant could be granted in a case where an obviously hot liquid like coffee or tea spills on a plaintiff because the hot liquid presents an open and obvious risk.

Huppe v. Twenty-First Century Restaurants of Am., Inc.[18]

CIRCUMSTANCES: The plaintiffs, Mr. and Mrs. Huppe, entered a McDonald's restaurant and purchased two large cups of coffee and a hamburger. The restaurant employee handed them lidded cups placed in a paper bag. The couple left the restaurant and returned to the car where Mrs. Huppe removed the coffee cup's lid to add cream and sugar. She was holding both cups in her hands when Mr. Huppe began backing the car out of its parking space. The car jerked and caused the coffee from both cups to spill onto the upper part of her body. Mr. Huppe parked, went into the restaurant, reported the burn, and asked for some water. He received a small cup, said it was not enough, and left the restaurant to tend to his wife. With help from a passerby, Mr. Huppe then

Although drinking a hot beverage while driving is common,
one sudden swerve or bump in the road may cause a spill
and second- or third-degree burns.

took his wife to a local hospital where she was treated for first- and second-degree burns to her chest, face, and shoulders.

CLAIMS: Products liability and breach of warranty: defective product (too hot), negligence, failure to warn

OUTCOME: The court decided that the coffee did not exceed the customary serving standards, there was no failure to warn because the coffee's hotness was contemplated and perceived by the plaintiff before she was injured, and there was no evidence that a warning would have permitted plaintiff to avoid or minimize injury. It was the sudden motion or jerking of the car and plaintiff's actions that caused the coffee to spill out of its cup.

The court concluded that as a matter of law the facts presented were insufficient evidence of claims to raise a triable issue of fact as to the liability of the defendant for plaintiff's injuries. The product was not defective or unusually dangerous, and there was no failure to warn. Therefore, the defendant was granted the motion for summary judgment dismissing the complaint.

Examples of Cases Settled without Trial

CASE A:
Beverage: Coffee, 16 oz., Styrofoam cup
Beverage temperature: Unknown
Spill environment: Driver's seat of the car, while driving, after leaving the drive-thru
Plaintiff involvement in spill: The beverage spilled while under control of the plaintiff
Activity that caused spill: Movement of the car
Burn area: Right ankle and right leg
Burn damage: Second degree

Plaintiff held the coffee in one hand as he drove because his car lacked cup holders that would accommodate the size of the cup. Coffee spilled onto his thigh when going over a bump in the road, which caused him to twist and jerk the cup away. The lid came off and dumped the coffee onto his lap.

CASE B:
Beverage: Latté
Beverage temperature: Unknown
Spill environment: Delivery surface at the café counter
Plaintiff involvement in spill: Plaintiff and employee were allegedly both holding the beverage
Activity that caused spill: Plaintiff's attempt to check how secure the lid was on the beverage
Burn area: Wrist
Burn damage: First- and second-degree burns

A server handed a latté to the plaintiff. It is unclear whether the plaintiff picked it up from the counter or it was handed to her by the server in mid-air. The plaintiff was burned on her right wrist as a result of trying to secure the cup's lid, which she claimed was not on correctly. The plaintiff suffered first- and second-degree burns that required skin grafts.

CASE C:
Beverage: Coffee, 16 oz. cup with sleeve and lid, 12 oz. cup with sleeve and lid
Beverage temperature: Unknown
Spill environment: Driver's seat of the car (stationary)
Plaintiff involvement in spill: The beverages were under control of the plaintiff
Activity that caused spill: Plaintiff's attempt to take beverages out of cup holders
Burn area: Thighs and groin
Burn damage: Second-degree burns

Plaintiff left both cups of coffee in the car's cup holders while running errands and before returning home. Upon her return, the plaintiff took both beverages in her hands, spilled some onto her thighs, and then dropped both cups onto her lap.

CASE D:
Beverage: Hot tea, 12 oz. cup
Beverage temperature: Unknown
Spill environment: Delivery counter surface inside café
Plaintiff involvement in spill: Allegedly did not touch the cup of tea prior to or during the spill
Activity that caused spill: poor service in delivering the drink (sliding it on the counter)
Burn area: Abdomen
Burn damage: First- and allegedly second-degree burns

A 12-oz. cup of tea spilled onto the plaintiff's abdomen from the delivery surface; it is unclear if the spill resulted due to server negligence (pushing the beverage toward the customer) or if the cup or lid deteriorated. There were no witnesses to the accident. An ambulance crew came to the scene and administered first aid, but the plaintiff refused to go to the hospital. Plaintiff did not claim that the temperature of the water exceeded industry standards, but did claim that the store employee was 100% negligent.

These are all cautionary tales. Ultimately, both court decisions and human trials of pain and suffering caused by hot beverage spills and burn injuries demonstrate that it does not serve anyone—plaintiff or defendant—to overlook or minimize the caution required when handling hot beverages. Airlines, hotels, hospital cafeterias, McDonald's, Starbucks, Dunkin' Donuts, 7-11, Burger King, trendy cafés, and convenience stores have all been called to the courtroom or negotiating table to account for hot beverage spills and grievous consumer burns. Consumers presume that this kind of scald burn is an anomaly—their beverage must have been defective and made inordinately, excessively, unreasonably hot. They claim the proprietor or server was negligent; they claim there was a failure to warn. But the hazards from a hot beverage spill are ubiquitous—the brewing temperatures are likely the same whether purchased from a cafe or when made in the kitchen while hunkered down at home.

From the cases analyzed in this chapter, as well as a number of other cases in my office files, the evidence demonstrates that the majority of spills occur when traveling with hot beverages in hand. These accidents don't often happen when people are at home and sitting still; they happen when people are busy and in motion, such as drivers of cars or passengers on airplanes. Lids pop-off from insecure fastening or jostles, bumps, and quick turns; spills occur when consumers remove lids to add condiments; cups drop when there is distracted or careless handling or when grabbed by a curious child's little hands. Rather than continuing to go to court to defend challenges to scientifically established brewing temperatures, it's time to change our focus. It's time to develop more effective methods for preventing hot beverage spills, and it is time to raise consumer awareness and caution by several degrees.

Citations

1. *Liebeck v. McDonald's Restaurants, P.T.S., Inc.*, No. CV-93-02419, 1995 WL 360309 (D.N.M. Aug. 18, 1994), vacated, 1994 WL 16777704 (D.N.M. Nov. 28, 1994).

2. *Hot Coffee*, Dir. Susan Saladoff. HBO, 2011. DVD.

3. "Frivolous" *Legal Information Institute*. Cornell University Law School, 19 Aug. 2010. Web. 25 February 2013. <www.law.cornell.edu/wex/frivolous>.

4. "How do People Attribute Blame for Burns Sustained from Hot

Coffee? The Causal Attributions," by Michael J. Kalsher, Gregory M. Phoenix, Michael S. Wogalter, Curt C. Braun, Proceedings of the Human Factors and Ergonomics Society Annual Meeting (1998), pp. 651-655, used by permission of *Sage Publications, Inc.*

5. *Holowaty v. McDonald's Corp.*, 10 F.Supp.2d 1078 (D. Minn. 1998

6. "Products Liability,"*Legal Information Institute.* Cornell University Law School, 19 Aug. 2010. Web. 25 February 2013. www.law. cornell.edu/wex/products_liability

7. *Colbert v. Sonic Restaurants, Inc.*, 741 F.Supp.2d 764 (W.D. La. 2010).

8. *Graham v. Yum Yum Donut Shop, Inc.*, No. BC515887, 2015 WL 10634748 (Super. Ct. Cal. Dec. 14, 2015).

9. *Lamkin v. Braniff Airlines, Inc.*, 853 F.Supp. 30 (D. Mass. 1994).

10. https://www.law.cornell.edu/wex/daubert_standard 4/4/18

11. *Mogavero v. Starbucks Corp.*, No. 2015-CA-003129, 2017 WL 2399154 (Fla. Cir. Ct. May 17, 2017).

12. *McCroy ex rel. McCroy v. Coastal Mart, Inc.*, 207 F.Supp.2d 1265 (D. Kan. 2002).

13. *Moltner v. Starbucks Coffee Co.*, No. 08 Civ. 9257, 2009 WL 3573190 (S.D.N.Y. Oct. 23, 2009), *affirmed*, 399 Fed.Appx. 630 (2d Cir. 2010).

14. *Wurtzel v. Starbucks Coffee Co.*, 257 F.Supp.2d 520 (E.D.N.Y. 2003).

15. *McMahon v. Bunn-O-Matic Corp.*, No. 3:96-CV-00538, 1997 WL 873829 (N.D. Ind. Nov. 10, 1997), *affirmed*, 150 F.3d 651 (7th Cir. 1998).

16. *Nadel v. Burger King Corp.*, 695 N.E.2d 1185 (Ohio Ct. App. 1997), *overruled by Bouher v. Aramark Services, Inc.*, 910 N.E.2d 40 (Ohio Ct. App. 2009).

17. *Bouher v. Aramark Services, Inc.*, 910 N.E.2d 40 (Ohio Ct. App. 2009).

18. *Huppe v. Twenty-First Century Restaurants of America, Inc.*, 497 N.Y.S.2d 306 (Sup. Ct. 1985).

CHAPTER TWO
Spill Prevention
Cups, Lids, Warnings, and Handling

In 1982, the tragic Tylenol capsule cyanide poisonings left seven people dead and sent shockwaves through the consumer products industry. It also prompted a revolution in product safety standards in the pharmaceutical and food industries. The United States Food and Drug Administration created regulations that required all retailers of non-prescriptions drugs to sell only products with tamper-evident and tamper-resistant packaging.

Tampering incidents in the 1980s also placed the food industry on high alert. Girl Scout cookies were found embedded with pins, needles, and other foreign objects; in 1989, bottles of Perrier water were contaminated with traces of benzene; baby food produced by leading manufacturers in both Great Britain and the U.S. discovered jars riddled with slivers of glass, razor blades, or caustic soda. What ensued in the heightened concern for consumer safety was the development and widespread use of safety caps, seals, and other tamper-resistant packaging—what began at the pharmacy with non-prescriptive drugs was soon followed by supermarket aisles with tamper-evident packaging for milk, soup, bottled water, ice cream, and more.

Great concern for consumer product safety also had taken the stage in 1965 when Ralph Nader's pioneering, bestseller book, *Unsafe at Any Speed: The Designed-In Dangers of the American Automobile,* shook the automotive industry. Nader charged that there was a gap between attainable safety and existing automotive designs. He argued there be a moral imperative for the industry to manufacture cars with engineered improvements to safeguard drivers and passengers. Although initially met by the industry with resistance and reluctance, Nader's clear and principled claim that more could be done to prevent serious injuries contributed to the creation of the National Highway Traffic Safety Administration, which eventually led to the evolution of seatbelts, crash tests, and other automotive safety features. Today, who would consider buying a car without airbags, seatbelts, and anti-lock brakes?

Certainly, it is likely that a hot beverage spill would yield less dramatic and fatal results than would a collision while driving an unsafe car without seatbelts; nonetheless, it is time to think about the common causes of hot beverage spills and to bridge the gaps between attainable safety and existing hot beverage container designs. Hot beverage scald burn victims have suffered second- and third- degree burns, endured significant pain and suffering, as well as repeated or lengthy hospitalizations, skin grafts, and permanent disfigurement. If hot beverage consumers were as painfully aware of the spill risks and hazards as burn victims now are, I daresay that in terms of issuing clearer warnings and containers designed to mitigate calamity—consumers' cost-to-benefit analysis would weigh-in for safety—even if the hot beverage cost a nickel more.

Guarding against Hazards

"A general tenet in human factors design is that safety should be ensured through the design of the system. If the potential hazard cannot be designed out, then it should be guarded against. If guarding against the hazard is not possible, then an adequate warning system should be developed."[1]

The first line of defense and protection from any dangerous aspect of a product is to eliminate the hazard. However, specific temperatures are intrinsic to the production and serving of hot beverages; lower brewing and holding temperatures change taste, aroma, and produce flavorless, unpalatable, warm drinks. Lowering serving temperatures to below the skin burn threshold would place teas and coffees well below most consumers' preferred drinking temperatures (as demonstrated in research shared in Chapter 3). Therefore, the temperature hazard cannot be designed out and maintain the quality of the beverage successfully.

Cups and Lids

The second line of defense and protection is to guard against the hazard. Because burns and hot beverage litigation have been the result of unintentional spills and not mouth burns from sipping and drinking, this responsibility requires examination of all other aspects of the serving environment for opportunities to guard against spills.

In hot beverage spill and burn lawsuits, the question of whether there was appropriate care taken to guard against the hazard relates to product liability or negligence claims of manufacturing or design defects. These issues concern the safe containment of hot liquids, such as cup thermal quality and stability, seam seals, and secure lids. To guard against spills and burns effectively, foodservice operators must ensure that both cup and lid quality are up to the task. Restaurant

Hot drinks to-go are served in disposable cups and lids in a range of styles with many variations. However, there are no industry-wide safety standards for cup and lid quality.

and foodservice operators usually purchase standard supplies from recognized manufacturers and assume that the proper research has been completed to see that the products are engineered for safety and stability. Product testing laboratories, such as Chicago Paper Testing Laboratory, Inc. (CPTL), among others, conduct product quality tests for manufacturers and foodservice companies. According to a CPTL company representative, all tests and pass-fail criteria are client specific. The tests are presently developed and dictated by the retailer or restaurant group. There are no manufacturing or industry standards for pass-fail. This is concerning. A lack of such industry standards compromises consumer safety and has legal implications as well. Coffee expert and former Executive Director of Specialty Coffee Association of America, Ted Lingle noted, "It is important for industry groups to set industry standards. Lack of standards from cup and lid manufacturers enormously complicated the defense of these [hot beverage spill and burn] cases."

Laboratory tests for cup and lid safety are valuable precautions. Cup and lid tests include, but are not limited to, the following assessments: seepage from seams and seals; a "tilt test" where a lidded cup is tilted and tested for drips, seepage, and lid fit; drop tests; cup inversions; compression tests for seepage through foam cup pores; and, a cup surface and internal beverage temperature test that plots change over time.

Heat can cause a consumer to drop and spill the contents of the cup; heat can weaken a cup's structural integrity. Cup stability is found or is found lacking in its design or manufacturing. Specific design elements for cup stability and safety include the following features: a cup base sufficient for the height and volume of hot contents; thermal quality that provides adequate hand insulation; shape and texture that is easy to grasp and hold securely when hot; and, the cup must have the structural integrity to safely contain hot contents at temperature over extended periods. Large to-go cups are susceptible to weakening from the temperature, weight, and volume of hot liquids, although poor design or faulty

CAUTION HOT!
HANDLE WITH CARE.

DO NOT MICROWAVE

This to-go cup has a removable sleeve to help protect hands from heat, but sleeves slip and fits vary. A better alternative is to use a well-insulated cup that doesn't require a sleeve.

manufacturing may cause cups of any size to weaken. (Cups designed for cold liquids should never be used for hot beverages.)

To-go cups are available as heat-resistant, insulated, lined, coated, rippled, air-pocketed, single-, double-, or triple-walled, etc. A strong, well-made, heat-resistant cup not only guards against a spill accident but also saves money and employee time by diminishing any perceived need to double-cup (placing the filled cup inside a second empty cup to provide extra heat/hand protection). Double-cupping is expensive for retailers and is a questionable practice. Although two cups may make the hot drink easier to hold, double-cupping may compromise lid alignment, lid-cup seal, and contribute to lid malfunctions. Coffee cup sleeves, such as Java Jackets, are another way to add a layer of thermal hand protection, and although helpful, they too are a less-than-ideal solution. Sleeves are not integrated into the manufacture of the cup itself and slip on and off too easily. Although it is common for many consumers to double-cup or use a sleeve for added hand protection, the safest choice is simply one strong, stable, thermal cup with better hand and beverage insulation.

The next consideration in guarding against the hazard from hot beverage spills is to make certain that the cup has a well made and securely fitted lid. This is imperative. All too many spill and burn lawsuits have cited lid failures or unintended lid pop-offs as the cause of the accident. Well-designed lids need to be easy to secure quickly and assuredly; they must have snug, sure-fitting seals that do not pop-off with the sloshing of hot liquid or with a drop, firm hand-squeeze, bump in the road, or air turbulence. The challenge to manufacturers is a contrary one: lids must be both quick and easy to secure for the speed of service and yet easy to remove for

Lids with white-on-white or black-on-black warnings
prove difficult to read and are likely to be ignored.

consumers to add sweeteners or dairy products; they must be able to be repeatedly and assuredly secured to avoid spills.

Since the introduction of the first flat-top, perforated opening lids of the 1970s, there have been some improvements: the peel back and click lid of the 1980s, the ubiquitous Solo Traveler lid in 1986, the domed lids with space for foamy lattes in the mid-1980s, and the Dart Optima resealable lid of the late 1990s, among others. The primary concern of these innovations was with improving consumers' sipping experience. More recently, lid and

An innovative new design by the *uVu Lids* company offers a double-inner seal that grips the inside of the cup for a more secure seal, small window slots for visual confirmation of a snug lid fit, and snap-shut sound. A deep reservoir also catches any overflow and prevent drips.

cup design engineers have begun to explore the use of new technology to improve both cup and lid safety and to advocate for its use. For example, in a white paper written by David Weiss, CEO of Uvutech (uVu Lids), "The Evolution of the Hot Beverage Lid: How we arrived at the current state of the art" he campaigned that lids should satisfy minimum laboratory tests, including those that measure the forces needed to pop a lid off from its cup, the forces needed to hold a lid onto a cup when passed or held only by the top and lid, and the forces needed for a lid to stay attached even when turned over, spilled, or dropped from a reasonable height. Further recommendations include that there be a method incorporated into the design for servers and consumers to quickly ascertain when the lid is properly seated, sealed, and safe to lift, tip, and drink. As Weiss noted, the issue of secure lids is of particular concern for quick-service restaurants and drive-through scenarios where employees are required to safely seat and seal hundreds of lids in a morning. The uVu lids' particular innovations include a double inner seal that grips the inside of the cup for a secure seal, four window slots along the rim for quick visual confirmation of a snug fit, a snap-shut sound, and a deep reservoir on the top of the lid to catch any overflow and help prevent drips.

Other manufacturers have also made innovations and contributions to cup and lid safety. Revocups, designed in Japan by Athena Kogyo Co., has introduced what it states is a spill-proof, disposable, lid-and-cup combo. The cup is matched with a locking lid and "turn-activated technology," which swivels the lid into open or closed positions. A light click sound indicates that the lid is open for sipping and with another twist, the lid will cover up the drinking cavity in its spill-proof position. Additionally, in a striking visual effort to raise consumer awareness that the beverage is hot and to handle with care, the Smart Lids has designed heat sensitive, color-changing coffee lids that turn bright red at temperatures above 118°F (48°C) and return to shades of coffee brown as the drink cools. Smart Lids also boasts a patented sealing indicator that shows when the lid is attached properly. MyLo Cool Lids has taken another approach and has created a lid with an insert. There is a top chamber that allows some of the hot beverage to cool faster while the beverage in the lower chamber is kept hot longer. The company claims that this design also increases cup stiffness and reduces the likelihood of spilling an entire cup.

Revocups, designed in Japan, has introduced a spill-proof, disposable
lid-and-cup combo featuring a turn-activated locking lid that
twists open and clicks shut for spill protection.

Reusable hot beverage containers, such as those manufactured
by Stanley and Lexo, have advanced their products too. They have
incorporated phase-changing temperature technology in stain-
less-steel tumblers to lower hot beverage temperatures from over
200°F to a modest temperature range of 130°–150°F and hold it
steady for hours. Reusable hot beverage cups present two good
problem-solving opportunities: they are safer thermal carriers of
hot liquids and offer a sustainable solution to the environmental
problem of disposable coffee cup waste.

In 2018, the Boston Tea Party café chain became the first sizable
company in Britain to announce a complete ban on disposable

cups. In an April 23, 2018 article written by Harry Cockburn in *The Independent*,[2] Boston Tea Party's Managing Director Sam Roberts reportedly said, "We will make this work, and we'll share the details of how we've done it with anyone who wants our help to do the same. We dream of a future where our children marvel at the fact that pre-2018 we would regularly use a cup once and throw it away."

Recently in the US, Berkley initiated single use cup fees and many cities across the US have banned polystyrene cups, including New York, Boston, Seattle, Baltimore, Miami, and Washington DC. Whether in Britain or the US, incentives to encourage the use of reusable thermal hot beverage containers would bring multiple benefits: cost savings for the retailer, spill prevention and safety for consumers, and environmental benefits for everyone.

Widespread marketplace use of reusable containers or sturdy to-go cups with locking, spill-proof lids would make a measurable difference in preventing hot drink spills and burns. The adoption of uniform minimum performance standards would help create and encourage the manufacturing and use of safer hot drink to-go packaging products. If only one recommendation from this book were to be adopted, tried and tested sturdy cups with locking lids should be the industry's priority. It's our first line of defense in guarding against hot beverage spills and avoiding burn lawsuits entirely.

Cup carriers and holders must also to be considered when guarding against hot beverage spills. When consumers order more than one beverage, they are commonly offered a heavy cardboard tray with indentations at the bottom to hold the cups in place. Other multiple cup carriers include a variety of slotted cardboard carrier sleeves and handled plastic bags specifically shaped to fit hot beverage cups. Also on the market are handled, cardboard,

Hand-to-hand transfer of hot beverages is never a safe or best practice.
The danger increases at drive-thrus where there isn't a counter to set the
tray down and cups and trays are handed off at a high-angled reach.

two-and four-cell carriers like those that carry a six-pack of soda
or beer.

Carrier trays may also help in difficult handling situations.
Consider the precarious handling challenges at a drive-thru
window—there is no way to avoid dangerous, mid-air, hand-to-
hand, hot drink transfers because there is no reachable counter
to set down or pick up hot drinks independently. The angle and
reach between drive-thru serving windows and customers' vehicles
vary betwixt and between a Mini Cooper, a Dodge mini-van, or
a lifted Ford F-150—by angle, by height, and by distance. More
prudent drive-thru serving options could, at minimum, utilize a
sturdy tray with deeply embedded cup holders for hand-offs, or
preferably, a slide-out drawer extending from the store window to

the vehicle (similar to those found at drive-through windows at some banks), or a stationary outside counter—all of which would help to eliminate the dodgy hand-to-hand cup transfer.

Handling hot beverages while operating a motor vehicle is common and concerning. Like touch-screen navigation, cell phone conversations, or fiddling with radios, driving with one hand on the wheel and a cup of hot liquid in the other can speedily contribute to a dangerous situation. The Department of Motor Vehicles considers there to be three types of distractions while driving: visual—taking your eyes off the road; manual—taking your hands off the wheel, and cognitive—taking your mind off driving.[3] Although most

The cardboard trays commonly used to serve multiple hot drinks
do not secure different cup sizes equally well.

modern cars provide some type and any number of cup holders, many are not designed well enough to avoid cup tip-overs and spills when negotiating the bumps, turns, quick starts or stops of ordinary road travel. Ford, however, has considered the issue and now has a patent for a self-leveling cup holder system designed to prevent a beverage from spilling while navigating turns or quick starts and stops.[4] Other gyroscopic cup-holders for use in vehicles have entered the marketplace but have yet to gain widespread use. However, no moving vehicle provides a safe situation for consumers to remove lids to add condiments safely.

Drive-thru convenience but another ill-advised hand-to-hand transfer of a scalding hot drink to an overtasked and distracted driver.

Passenger safety is the number one concern for airline pilots
and crews, but this awareness and vigilance does not yet
extend to handling hot drinks safely in flight.

Other modes of travel also compound the hazards for safe
handling of hot beverages. Airlines and passengers are vulnerable.
Airlines often serve unlidded cups of hot beverages that are passed
hand-to-hand, across a row of passengers, and placed on fold-down
tray tables. There are no adequate cup holders nor tray indentations
deep enough for an unlidded cup to remain upright and stead-
fastly survive a knee-jerk, an elbow, a backward reclining seat, or
air-pocket turbulence.

For many people, flying on a commercial airline has become a
dreaded event. The security lines, vying for overhead luggage space,
paying for extras that used to be free, (checked baggage, blankets,

If you spilled a cup of hot coffee or tea on your lap mid-flight,
how easy might it be and how long might it take to reach
the bathroom for wet, cool, cloths and burn/pain relief?

pillows) have added to the angst and hassle of flying. In addition, planes have become smaller in size and personal seat space more limited, less comfortable, and many flights are packed near-to-full passenger capacity.

When it comes to in-flight beverage service, the offerings remain much the same. In the first-class section there are many options, but in coach class, there are just a few. But among the universal offerings are hot coffee and tea.

Making coffee on an airplane is more difficult due to the atmospheric cabin pressure around 6,500 feet altitude, which remains constant throughout a flight. This means the temperature to brew coffee is lower than it is at sea level—about 180-190°Fahrenheit (82.2–87.8°C) vs. the industry standard of 195-205°Fahrenheit (90.5–96.1°C). Hot enough to be tolerable for most passengers but not hot enough to maximize flavors that are released at higher temperatures.

Coffee is brewed in the cabin kitchen, held in a pot or thermal carafe, and then served in a cup and handed to the passenger. In first class, coffee is usually served in a ceramic mug with a handle. The coffee is not lidded and can be placed on a tray table or in a console between the seats. In coach class, coffee is often served in a paper cups and handed to the passenger unlidded. Any requested condiments (sugar packets or individual creamers) are handed to the person along with the hot drink. If the passenger is in an inside seat, either in a multi-seat row (five across) or a window seat (three across), the hand-off becomes quite perilous. The flight attendant has to reach across several passengers with a cup of very hot liquid, and the recipient has to secure the unlidded cup and place it on a tray table that may or may not have a slight circle depression to indicate the cup can be placed at that location. These depressions are nowhere near adequate to prevent tip-overs and spills.

Hot beverages as presently served on most airlines loom as accidents-waiting-to-happen. The spill and burn opportunities are many. Here are some common and ever-hazardous scenarios: one,

A slight indentation on a movable tray is not a safe and secure cup holder. An airplane's normal flight will include banked turns, passengers' elbows or seat movements, and occasional turbulence.

the plane hits a pocket of rough air, and the flight attendant drops or spills the coffee on a passenger; two, a passenger in the row moves as the flight attendant attempts to reach across to deliver coffee to another passenger and causes the hot drink to spill; three, a passenger in the row in front of the receiving passenger suddenly decides to recline his/her seat during the hand-off or, when the cup is perched on the tray there is turbulence and the hot drink spills. Lastly, children on planes do what all children do; they are curious and they wiggle and squirm. They may topple a cup on a tray or jostle the beverage cart parked in the aisle and spill a substantial quantity of scalding liquid.

Here are two recent spill and burn lawsuits that illustrate some of the common hazards encountered when serving hot beverages to passengers on airlines:

According to a 2017 article by Dean Balsamini in the *New York Post*,[5] a JetBlue passenger suffered from a hot tea spill during a flight to Las Vegas when a flight attendant apparently failed to secure the lid. The tea spilled when the passenger bumped the tray table and resulted in second- and third-degree burns to her bottom. The passenger claimed it "wasn't fit for human consumption" and was "capable of causing disfiguring burns." She was reported saying, "I was in excruciating pain and had tears running down my eyes and asked them to get me anything." She claimed the flight attendants thought she was "insane" for complaining, but eventually offered aspirin and ice. It was only after she pulled down her pants to show the crew that they took her complaints seriously and offered to meet her at the gate with a stretcher.

In another incident, reported by NBC News,[6] Willard Shepard wrote that a passenger on Republic Airlines (contracted by American Airlines) suffered third-degree burns to her abdomen and breasts when a flight attendant offered her an unlidded cup of coffee and spilled it on her before it was in her hands. Her lawyer was reported as saying that there was no turbulence and commented that "I don't see why they are offering coffee at such high temperatures...At a minimum, they should have been serving the coffee with a secure lid. It could happen to anybody."

A complication arises when any airline passenger has spilled a hot beverage on themselves. For the passenger to go to the restroom for clean-up or burn relief, the person has to unbuckle a seatbelt, muddle by other passengers seated in the row, scramble down the aisle (which may be blocked by the beverage cart or other passengers) before reaching the restroom, which may or not be occupied. This effort will take precious time and much more time than the mere seconds it takes for hot liquids to cause severe burns. Not a good situation. Flight attendant training should include first-aid treatment for scald burns because the appropriate treatment requires immersing the burn area in cool water or wrapping in clean, cool, wet cloths—it does not include applying ice, salves, or offering aspirin as commonly assumed and demonstrated in the JetBlue flight attendant's response described above.

These situations cry for change. Airlines should be made more aware of the hazards and respond with the use of cups with locking lids, secure cup holders for trays or seats, and, of course, written and verbal warnings to remind passengers to handle with care. To further minimize potential spill and burn risks, all hot beverages offered in moving public conveyances, such as airplanes, trains, ferry boats, or buses, should be fully prepared by the server and the quantity limited to 5-6 ounces of hot liquid in 8-ounce securely lidded cups. Staff should also be trained in appropriate first-aid care for scald burns. Whether on air, sea, or land, all vehicles used for passenger travel should be equipped with safe and well-designed cups, lids, and cup-holders to better accommodate hot beverages and travelers in motion.

Warnings

The third defense to protect the public from danger is to warn the consumer about the product hazard. Failure to warn is another common claim in many hot beverage product liability lawsuits—despite most consumers demonstrable familiarity with drinking hot beverages. The disconnect between consumers' familiarity regarding hot beverages and their lack of familiarity about the severe burns that can result from spills is alarming.

Clearly, existing cup and lid warnings have not sufficed. Cautionary warnings are commonly printed on the cups and are embossed on the lids. Warnings printed on cups vary greatly in content, placement, and size. Warnings embossed on lids are difficult to read as they are in the same color as the lid—white letters on white lids or black on black. Because litigants commonly claim that the warnings were inadequate to make known the serious scald burns possible from hot beverage spills, it is imperative to design hot beverage spill warnings that are more visible and make the hazard unmistakably clear.

The continued "failure to warn" claims should be the industry's risk management call-to-action. Stronger, easily recognizable hazard warnings can replace the haphazard and inconsistent warnings presently found on cups and lids. They should heed the American National Standards Institute (ANSI) recommendations for product safety warnings—highly visible, familiar icons with succinct, unambiguous terminology. Secondary written warnings could also be posted at point of purchase counters and drive-thru windows: "Warning: Handle with Care! Hot Beverage Spills can Cause Serious Burns." Further, written notices could be reinforced with a server's verbal warning at the time of sale: "Careful! That coffee/tea/cocoa is very hot and can cause serious burns if spilled." This is similar to warnings given by restaurant servers to diners when presenting meals on very hot plates. Incorporating

Lots of warning messages and good intentions, but are the messages readable and clear, consistent and compelling? Do you know what they urge you to do?

these three suggestions would help to ensure that consumers have been judiciously warned: three times, in three places, and in three different manners. The retailer is diligent. There would be no failure to warn.

Effective Warnings

A short, simple, expressive hazard warning must accomplish three things: (1) attract attention, so the consumer notices and encodes the warning, (2) inform, so the consumer comprehends the warning, and (3) motivate, so the consumer complies with the warning.[1]

Warning psychology literature states that an effective warning must be clear about the purpose of the warning and the effectiveness in accomplishing specific objectives.[7] An effective and motivating warning message would precipitate a positive response to the question "Does this product threaten the average consumer and compel him or her to use the product responsibly?" The motivational impact of a warning is measured by how effective it is at attracting attention, informing the consumer of risks, and its success in eliciting the requested response of more cautious behavior.

Currently, most hot beverage warnings just caution the consumer that the contents are hot, but this generic language makes it difficult to evaluate the warning's success or failure in eliciting more cautious handling. We know that consumers expect their coffee, tea, and cocoa to be served hot, but we do not know whether existing warnings are noticed and the hazard truly comprehended. Further, we do not know whether consumers have been sufficiently urged and motivated to comply with the warning. When the warning simply states "Caution: Beverage is Hot," consumers may wonder: Why would you tell me that hot coffee/tea/cocoa is hot? I know that.

When a more explicit warning is presented in conjunction with a specific recommended response, the purpose of the warning is

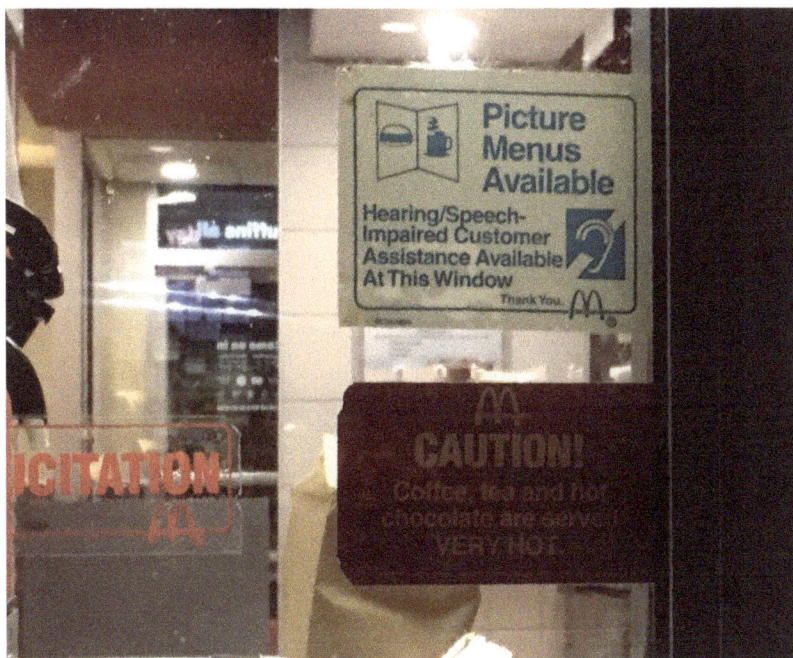

The brown poster warning caution at a drive-through window is a step in the right direction. There should be clear, consistent, safety warnings given in multiple ways: on cups, lids, signage posters at the point of purchase, and verbal warnings given to customers at the hand-off.

made clear to the consumer. For example, Warning—Handle with Care—Hot beverage spills can cause serious burns. Specificity makes the hazard and the required response obvious. It also makes it easier to determine whether the warning was effective by whether consumers altered behavior accordingly (such as checking whether the lid is secure or adding condiments at the counter before leaving).

Warning Components

The tools used to create warnings include signal words, recognizable symbols or pictorial images, distinguishing colors, readable fonts, and visible placement.

Ideally, hot beverage warnings should be placed on the cup and the lid; the signal word and warning symbol should be noticeable and prominent; the typography, font size, and colors should be legible and stand out from the background. The placement of a warning has been shown to influence all steps of the warning process.[1] However, the placement of warnings on hot beverage cups poses a challenge—the warning must remain visible to the consumer while holding the cup. Warnings on lids might be more visible and more widely read, but only when the product is lidded and the warning presented in attention-grabbing colors.

Signal Words

ANSI issues guidelines for product safety signs and labels. The organization uses three signal words to classify and communicate hazards, level of risk, and severity of harm: Caution, Warning, and Danger.[8]

A signal word is selected according to the risk of harm presented by the hazardous situation. That is, signal word selection is based on the risk posed if the safety message is not followed.

The risk is determined by the following criteria:

• Worst credible severity of harm if accident occurs;
• Probability of an accident if the hazardous situation occurs (i.e., if the safety message is not followed);
  • Probability of the worst credible severity of harm occurring

DANGER: Indicates the imminently hazardous situation, which if not avoided, will result in death or severe injury. This signal word is limited to use in the most extreme situations.

WARNING: Indicates a potentially hazardous situation, which if not avoided, could result in death or severe injury. Injury to humans that is more severe than minor or moderate injury.

CAUTION: Indicates a potentially hazardous situation that, if not avoided, may result in minor or moderate injury. It may also be used to alert against unsafe practices.

Serious injuries typically have one or more of the following characteristics:

• Results in permanent loss of function or significant disfigurement
• Requires substantial and prolonged medical treatment
• Involves long periods of disability
• Involves considerable pain and suffering over long periods of time
• Examples of serious injuries include amputations, severe burns, and loss or impairment of vision or hearing.

Moderate or minor injury is classified as "injury to humans, not including death or serious injury. Harm classified as moderate or minor injury may also include property damage that occurs as a result of the same event. Minor or moderate injuries do not typically result in disability or significant disfigurement or pain. Examples of minor or moderate injuries include cuts, scratches, and irritation." [8]

Presently, the signal word "CAUTION" is typically and voluntarily used in hot beverage warnings, but it should be replaced by the stronger signal word "WARNING" as befits the level of hazard (severe injury) per ANSI standards under the terms of Z535.4 of Signal Word Selection.

Symbols and Safe Responses

Written warnings are usually accompanied by easily recognizable symbols or pictorial images that convey universal meanings and help to avoid language or literacy barriers. The presence of a recognizable image allows people to identify the presence of a warning more quickly. Pictorial or symbolic representation can be used effectively as stand-alone warnings or in conjunction with a written warning. In terms of encoding, comprehension, and compliance, symbols are most effective when accompanied by written information. Pictorials are explicit visual descriptions of the concept in an image such as steam or the flames of fire; symbols are abstract representations with a clear correlation to what they signify, such as exclamation points for "pay attention" or a red circle with a crossed line for "No" or "don't." The meaning is learned.

"An Investigation of Preferred Shapes for Warning Labels,"[9] conducted by Riley, Cochran, and Ballar independently examined nineteen different shapes to determine which were most likely to attract attention. The researchers found that "the triangle on its vertex was the preferred warning indicator among the shapes tested."

To date, symbols or pictorial images have not been consistently included with written hot beverage hazard warnings; however, we encourage our industry to implement this change as research and warning literature substantiate that incorporating an image into a hazard warning helps attract attention and increases visibility.

Participants in studies have shown that succinct, explicit warnings are perceived as indicative of greater hazard.[1] More specific hot beverage warnings would help to increase consumer awareness, and they might also help mitigate product liability and design defect claims where plaintiffs state they were not adequately warned that a spill could cause serious burns.

Explicit warnings are not lengthy and detailed warnings. To be effective, the hazard and the required response must be specific and succinct. Explicit warnings are clear, to the point, and avoid industry-specific or medical jargon. To date, most hot beverage warnings warn in modest print that the beverage is hot and state that it should be handled with care. At first, this information seems logical and warning enough, but repeated spill calamities show that this warning has not sufficed. Court rooms and hospital rooms have made clear that more explicit warnings are required to effectively raise consumer awareness about the dangers of careless handling and hot beverage spills. It calls for a patently unmistakable statement, such as, "Hot Beverage Spills can Cause Severe Burns."

Compliance with the warning also increases if the warning details a safe response.[1] This gives the reader clear instructions regarding what they must do to avoid the hazard. In the hot beverage industry, a provided response that detailed the multiple ways someone could spill or avoid spilling a beverage would be long and verbose. It certainly would not fit on a cup. A distilled requested response that would fit on cups or lids is "HANDLE with CARE!" Additionally, interactive warnings have been shown to increase noticeability, encoding, and compliance.[1] The Smart Lid company's color-changing lid (red to brown) along with its visual indicators that show whether the cup/did seal is safely secured is an example of an interactive warning with the added benefit of lid-seal safety features.[10] Additionally, recognition that product familiarity and warnings can lead to habituation and inattention, some policymakers have required multiple and varied warnings that are rotated among packages and advertisements in another effort to increase consumer notice, comprehension, and compliance.

⚠ WARNING

Hot beverage spills can cause severe burns! Handle with care.

At present, hot beverage warnings are a voluntary effort and are haphazard in both use and design. We urge industry stakeholders to consistently use warnings on hot beverage containers that are informed by warning literature recommendations and ANSI guidelines. These warnings would include a strong visual symbol (such as a yellow triangle with a steam-rising cup and/or an exclamation point), the signal word (Warning), followed by a provided response (Handle with Care!) and the specific danger (Hot Beverage Spills can Cause Severe Burns). Prudent risk managers could presage failure-to-warn claims in litigation by issuing multiple and varied warnings, including the addition of ANSI-informed warnings on all hot beverage cups or lids.

Caveat Emptor: Consumer Variables and Warning Compliance

Social scientists, as well as marketing and other communication specialists, have long recognized that people's responses to information and motivational messages are not uniform—this, in turn, translates to the fact that noticing a warning does not ensure compliance. Many variables play a role in a consumer's response to warnings: previous experiences, hazard perception, risk tolerance, age, literacy, vision, etc. Accommodation of all consumer variables to ensure compliance would be impossible. Lawyers and consumers cannot assume that management of all such variables is within the purveyors' control.

In David Stewart and Ingrid Martin's article in the *Journal of Public Policy and Marketing*, "Intended and Unintended Consequences of Warning Messages: A Review and Synthesis of Empirical Research,"[11] we stated, "Behavior change is not a useful measure of [warning] attention because behavior is influenced by many factors other than attention. That a consumer does not respond to a warning does not necessarily imply that the message has failed to gain attention. A consumer may well attend to a warning but reject its message because he or she does not believe it, or the cost of compliance is perceived as greater than the benefit."

We also noted that "The perceived hazard associated with a product, in turn, has been shown to decline with increasing familiarity with the product (Godfrey et al. 1983)." This is quite pertinent for the hot beverage industry and for the many cases where daily coffee drinkers claim they are shocked by the burns and harm sustained from a spill. Stewart and Martin go on to say "Similarly, Robinson (1977) suggests that individuals with prior product experience may be more likely to ignore warning information because they have not had accidents in the past. Avoidance of accidents may decrease the perceived risk associated with the product."

This is a typical and troublesome hand-to-hand transfer—mid-air, holding the cup from the top, and a cross-body reach to navigate the cup to the holder in the console.

Do most daily coffee drinkers know and believe that a hot drink spill could burn through three layers of skin and down to the bone within seconds? Not many, not likely, not yet. In handling hot beverages, consumers' familiarity with the product and its frequent, safe use has played a noteworthy role in overlooked caution and warnings. Familiarity can both lead to a greater understanding of the risks associated with the product, or it can inure consumers to its dangers. An example can be seen with cars and drivers—some drivers become more careful as they learn more about the inherent dangers of driving a car and wear seatbelts, observe speed limits, streetlights, and warning signs; other drivers become desensitized with regular use and grow careless, speed, never yield way, run lights, or otherwise drive more recklessly. Similarly, it seems that frequent and safe experiences drinking hot beverages may have desensitized many consumers to the inherent hazards of a spill. Consumers underestimate the risks and do not heed the numerous and ineffective existing warnings.

Warning compliance increases when there is an increased perception of hazard.[1] If consumers expect to encounter a dangerous product, they are more apt to look for, notice, comprehend, and comply with a warning. The opportunity exists for the hot beverage industry to increase consumer awareness and hazard perception through the creation and use of multiple and more effective warnings. At present, consumers' perception of hot beverage spill and burn hazard is low and existing cautionary warnings are perpetually ignored. Our industry's countering response must be pervasive, persuasive, and clear:

Safe Handling

Handling hot drinks with care pertains to servers as well as consumers. There are ways to hand a hot beverage to a customer that greatly reduce the risk of contents spilling, which is detailed in the final chapter, "Best Practice Recommendations for Commercial Operations." In sum, the safe transfer of cup from the server to the customer should never be passed from hand-to-hand: a securely lidded cup should be placed down on a stable, smooth, level surface for the customer to pick up from the counter independently. Servers should never slide beverages across any table surface or counter. The momentum of the cup and the potential for the cup to become caught on an uneven or sticky surface greatly increases spill risk. Servers also should not place a hot beverage directly into a customer's hands; this avoids any missed non-verbal cues that might result in one or the other person dropping the cup.

The way the beverage is served also gives rise to the question of whether the establishment or the customer should secure the lid on the cup. On the one hand, if the customer is satisfied with an unaltered beverage, placing a securely lidded cup on the counter for them to pick up eliminates the need for any fiddling with the lid. However, when customers add their condiments, handing them a lidded beverage invokes more precarious handling when they remove and reseal the lid. Unlidded beverages pose significant safety risks, particularly for consumers in moving vehicles such as airplanes and cars. For safety concerns, I urge that all beverages served for travel—drive-thrus, take-out, or on trains, ferries, or airplanes—be prepared by the server with requested condiments and then served lidded. Whether in response to safety concerns or material management and efficiencies, some foodservice operators have already opted to place any requested sweeteners or dairy products in the drink on the customer's behalf before placing the lid on and serving. Although it is a somewhat more labor intensive and service-oriented route, serving lidded hot beverages alleviates the need for customers to remove and replace lids, and thereby also removes one of the riskiest elements of handling hot drinks safely.

This image shows the best way to deliver a hot beverage to the customer. The server (left) places a lidded cup down on the counter for the customer (right) to pick up independently. There is no opportunity for missed non-verbal cues or clumsy hand-to-hand maneuvers.

Conclusion

Manufacturers should design and produce disposable and reusable containers that are effective and economically viable for serving hot drinks safely. To-go carriers for multiple beverages must be redesigned to better accommodate large cups securely. Foodservice operators should train staff to handle hot beverages safely, issue consumer warnings, serve only prepared beverages to travelers and children, and purchase cups and lids that meet safety guidelines. Airlines and other public transportation should serve small quantities of prepared hot beverages in cups with secure locking lids and provide travelers with adequate cup holders. Drive-thrus should develop a better means for safe conveyance of hot beverages to vehicles.

Industry trade associations should align to set standards for product safety. The lack of consistent safety standards for cup and lid manufacturers undermines quality assurance for serving hot beverages safely; a lack of consistent and clear warnings contributes to consumers' dearth of hazard awareness when handling hot beverages. We strongly recommend that the National Coffee Association, Specialty Coffee Association, and the National Restaurant Association collaborate to create industry standards for to-go cups, lids, carriers, and warnings, as well as best practice guidelines and training materials for the safe handling of hot beverages to consumers.

Then, once we are confident that we've done what is within our power to ensure that hot drinks are safely contained and delivered with a cautionary warning, it is pursuant that consumers take responsibility for their actions and heed our loud and clear wake-up call: Warning! Hot Beverage Spills can Cause Severe Burns. Please—Handle with Care.

Summary: Spill Prevention

Create Industry Standards

✓ We strongly recommend that the National Coffee Association, Specialty Coffee Association, and the National Restaurant Association collaborate to create industry standards for to-go cups, lids, carriers, and warnings, as well as best practice guidelines and training materials for the safe handling of hot beverages to consumers.

Cup and Lid Quality Assurance

✓ Cups and lids should meet established industry safety standards for hot liquid containment.

✓ Cups should be of high quality, double-walled, or another insulating feature that ensures the surface is not too hot to handle. There should be no need for double-cupping or sleeves.

✓ Lids should lock closed and have features that allow for confirmation of a secure closure (an audible snap, windows to view the seal, or an interior cup lid/rim seal).

Warnings, Warnings, Warnings

✓ ANSI-informed warnings on to-go cups that alert consumers with written text and visual images:

⚠ WARNING

Hot beverage spills can cause severe burns! Handle with care.

- ✓ Warning hazard signs at all points of sale, including drive-thru windows

- ✓ Verbal warnings given by all staff when serving hot drinks to customers "Be Careful! This drink is hot, and spills can cause serious burns."

Serving Hand-off

- ✓ All to-go hot drinks served at drive-thru windows or on methods of public conveyance (such as airlines), should be prepared and lidded with customers' requested condiments, unless the customer demands otherwise. In that situation, the customer should be warned once again to "Handle with Care: Hot beverage spills can cause serious burns."

- ✓ All hot drinks should be placed down on a counter for the customer to pick up independently. There should be no hand-to-hand delivery of hot drinks. No sliding hot beverages across counters. Multiple drinks should be served in a purposeful, secure, stable tray for delivery.

- ✓ Airlines should have tray tables that hold hot beverage cups securely to keep them from spilling during turbulence, passenger movements, or a fellow traveler's reclining seat in the row ahead.

Serving Hot Beverages to Children

- ✓ Do not serve hot beverages to young children who are traveling on airplanes or in cars: no hot cocoa, hot tea, or coffee. Period. If served to an accompanying adult, the hot drink should be served with a clear and specific hazard warning.

Staff Training

- ✓ Educate all employees on the burn risks of spilled hot beverages to foster a spill-free environment.

- ✓ Train servers how to safely prepare and present hot beverages to customers.

- ✓ Ensure that all employees are thoroughly trained to handle hot beverage spills, including Good Samaritan first aid and incident reports.

- ✓ Ensure that emergency response and first aid posters are prominently displayed, first aid kits are well stocked, and cool water is at hand. Include clean, small hand towels or face cloths in a zip-lock bag for use when a burn injury cannot be immersed under a running faucet or in the sink.

Citations

1. Wendy A. Rogers, Nina Lamson, and Gabriel K. Rousseau. "Warning Research: An Integrative Perspective." *Human Factors* Vol. 42.1, pp.102-139, (2000)

2. Harry Cockburn, "Coffee chain becomes first to announce complete ban on disposable cups," *The Independent*, April 23,2018 https://www.independent.co.uk/environment/disposable-coffee-cup-ban-plastic-waste-boston-tea-party-sam-roberts-a8319071.html

3. https://www.dmv.org/distracted-driving/three-types-of-distractions.php

4. https://www.cnet.com/roadshow/news/fords-self-leveling-cup-holder-keeps-your-coffee-safe-at-speed/

5. https://nypost.com/2017/09/02/jetblue-burned-my-butt-with-hot-tea-lawsuit/

6. https://www.nbcmiami.com/news/local/Coffee-Badly-Burns-Woman-During-Flight-to-Miami-Attorney-440823153.html

7. David W. Stewart and Ingrid M. Martin, "Intended and Unintended Consequences of Warning Messages: A Review and Synthesis of Empirical Research," *Journal of Public Policy & Marketing*, Vol 13 Spring 1994, 1-19

8. American National Standards Institute (ANSI) American National Standard Product Safety Signs and Labels, ANSI Z535.4 2007 Reprinted by permissionof the National Electrical Manufacturers Association

9. Michael W. Riley, David J. Cochran, John L. Ballard "An Investigation of Preferred Shapes for Warning Labels" *Human Factors* Vol 24, Issue 6, pp. 737-742 http://journals.sagepub.com/doi/abs/10.1177/001872088202400610

10. "Smart Lid – Disposable Color Changing Coffee Cup Lids," Smart Lid Active Beverage Packaging. N.p.,n.d. Web.17 Nov. 2012 http://www.smartlid.com/.

CHAPTER THREE

Matters of Degree

Brewing Temperatures & Scald Burns

The hot beverage industry has flourished because of its untiring quest to produce high-quality drinks that consumers enjoy. Although the process of making a good cup of coffee or tea may seem simple, many variables must be handled well to successfully achieve—and safely deliver—an appealing and flavorful cup to the consumer repeatedly.

Brewed coffee and tea are typically about 98.5-99% water—essentially flavored water—but when taste and aromatic compounds are properly extracted from tea leaves or coffee beans, hot water is transformed into one of the world's two most favored hot drinks. Unlocking the flavor secrets of good coffee and tea has come from a wealth of experience and solid research. The hot beverage industry's best practice recommendations for brewing, holding, and serving drinks reflect decades of careful scientific study and consensus. Chemical analysis and sensory evaluations substantiate the specific temperatures necessary to brew a properly extracted cup of hot coffee or tea.

Brewing Temperatures

The development of coffee's intrinsic flavors (aroma and taste) are released when raw coffee beans are roasted. Roasted coffee beans are ground before brewing to increase the surface area by reducing the particle size, which allows for more efficient and effective extraction of soluble flavor compounds during brewing. The coffee brewing process has three stages: wetting, hydrolysis, and extraction, however, for the purposes of this chapter, the focus will be on the relationship of beverage quality as it pertains to water brewing temperatures and flavor extraction.

Brewing Temperatures of Consumer Coffee Makers			
Maker	Keurig	Ninja	Cuisinart 14-cup
Brew Temperature	200°F	205°F	200°F

The brewing process infuses roasted coffee grounds in hot water. Because water usually accounts for about 98.5-99% of the finished brew, it is critical for the water to be pH neutral, the proper temperature, and the right volume. When heated to between 195-205°F (90.5-96.1°C), the signature aromas and tastes are correctly extracted from the coffee grounds. It is a precise set of conditions: if the water temperature is too cool, not enough flavor will extract, and the lower temperature will create thin, under-extracted coffee; if the water temperature is too high, the grounds burn and produce a flat, astringent, sour, or bitter brew and over-extracted coffee. Because water temperature has such significant impact on beverage profile and quality, this range has become the industry's best practice recommendation for both commercial and consumer coffee-brewing machines.

This coffee brewing temperature recommendation was established by the Coffee Brewing Center of the Pan-American Coffee Bureau through the research of Dr. Earl Lockhart in 1952.[2] During sensory analyses, the temperature range of 195-205°F (90.5-96.1°C), was determined to produce the most pleasing balance of acidity, body, bitterness, and astringency.[2,3] Although acidity and body

Mr. Coffee 10-cup	Black + Decker 12-cup	Hamilton Beach 12-cup	OXO On 9-cup	Braun KF7150BK
203°F	196°F	190°F	203°F	189°F

are considered desirable traits, bitterness and astringency are not. Chemical analyses of coffee brewed at different temperatures also confirm the sensory findings: there are significant differences in the chemical composition of coffees brewed at different temperatures.[3]

Brewing Temperatures of Consumer Coffee Makers*

Brand	Model	Brew Temperature	Holding Temperature
Bonavita	BV1800	195-205°F	-
Techni Vorm	Moccamaster	200°F	175-185°F
Hammacher Schlemmer	Bitterness Eliminating Coffee Maker	200°F	-
Cloer	5218NA	200°F	-
Behmor Inc.	Brazen	190-210°F	-
Mr Coffee	BVMC-PSTX91	Up to 205°F	-
Ratio	Eight	202°F	-
Chemex	Ottomatic	197.6-204.8°F	176-185°F
Kitchen Aid	Pour Over Coffee Brewer	200°F	-

*Temperatures as derived from the operating manuals

Brewing Temperatures of Commercial Coffee Makers

Brand	Model	Brew Temperature
Zojirushi	CD-LTC50	195°F (default), up to 208°F
Fetco	CBS-2031/32	200°F (default), 180-208°F
BUNN	FMD/A DBC-3	195°F
Curtis	TP2T/TP2S	200°F

Brewing Temperatures of Commercial Water Boilers for Tea

Brand	Model	Holding Temperature
Zojirushi	CD-LTC Commercial Water Boiler and Warmer	208°F, 195°F, or 175°F

The steeping process for hot teas involves the immersion of loose tea leaves, pressed tea cakes, or a teabag in hot water that has first been brought to a full boil from cold. The type of tea determines the recommended steeping temperatures—the larger and more delicate the leaf, the lower the water temperature. Black teas are infused directly from a rolling boil, but a white leaf tea will scorch at that temperature. For black teas, the industry literature and trade associations (including the UK Tea and Infusions Association and Tea Association of the USA), recommend the use of freshly drawn water at or between 203-212°F (95-100°C) for optimal flavor extraction from leaves.[4] Oolongs and white teas are brewed between 180-190°F (82.2-87.7°C). Because of its more delicate nature, green tea leaves require lower steeping temperatures to avoid the bitterness that occurs if steeped at higher temperatures. Green teas should be made with water that has cooled from boiling to 155-195°F (68.3-90.5°C), depending on variety. Finally, herbal infusions, also known as *tisanes*, have higher recommended steeping temperatures of 212°F (100°C).

Although there are no mandated standards for brewing hot coffee or tea, there are published *Recommendations for the*

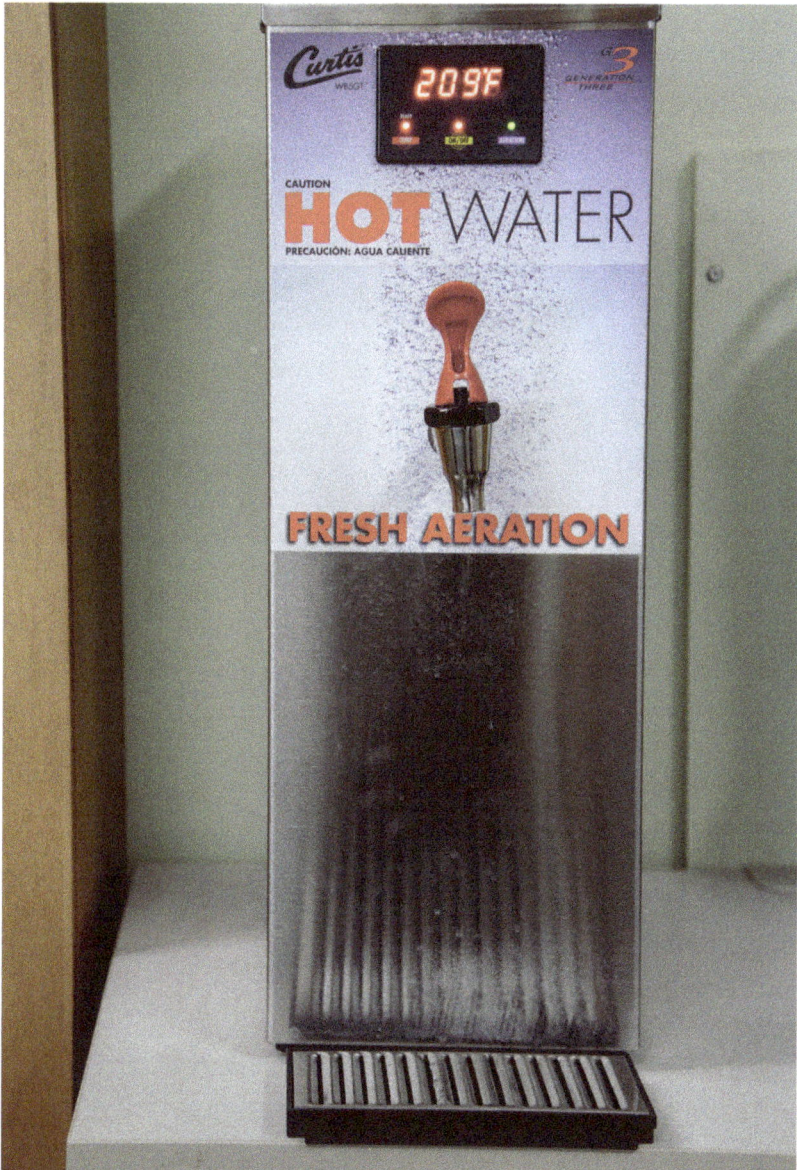

This is a commercial hot water dispenser at a temperature common for making teas, some cocoas, and instant soups.

Preparation of Iced and Hot Tea by the Tea Association of the USA, Inc. (published in cooperation with the National Restaurant Association)[4] and there is the Specialty Coffee Association's Golden Cup Standard.[5] These are voluntary consensus standards for best practices, which are well-researched and published recipes, procedures, and protocols that are widely accepted and shared by many industry experts. None of the recommended temperatures for brewing, holding, or serving beverages are uninformed, subjective, or haphazard. Nor have the temperatures suddenly increased over time to surprisingly become excessively hot, as some litigants claim. Indeed, in recent years manufacturers of home coffeemakers have raised brewing temperatures to that of commercial enterprises in response to consumer demand that their coffee be as flavorful and hot.

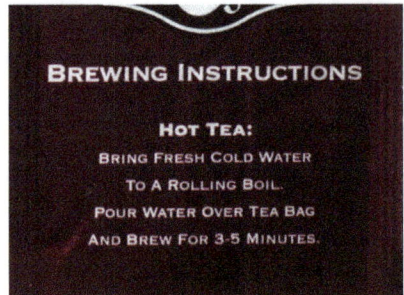

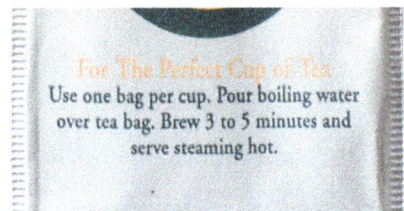

FOR BEST STEEPING

Bring fresh filtered water to a boil

Pour over pyramid sachet

Steep for 3-5 minutes

BREWING INSTRUCTIONS

HOT TEA:
BRING FRESH COLD WATER TO A ROLLING BOIL.
POUR WATER OVER TEA BAG AND BREW FOR 3-5 MINUTES.

212°F   2-5 min.

For The Perfect Cup of Tea
Use one bag per cup. Pour boiling water over tea bag. Brew 3 to 5 minutes and serve steaming hot.

Tea is usually brewed at higher temperatures than coffee. Coffee is made at 195-205°F (90.5-96°C); boiling water for tea is 212°F (100°C).

Hot Cocoa

Cocoa also falls under the umbrella of hot beverages that can burn when spilled. But there are differences and elements that beg closer review: Who are its customers? What are the suitable temperatures? Are there hot cocoa industry standards?

In one of the lawsuits cited in the previous chapter, an eleven-year-old boy suffered first- and second-degree burns when he spilled his to-go hot cocoa while riding in his mother's car. His beverage was made from a convenience store's instant powder cappuccino machine. In another incident, a seven-year-old girl was badly burned when she was served hot cocoa at a to-go foodservice franchise. This company's serving policy was to hand the hot chocolate packet, a stir stick, and a cup of hot water (taken from the coffee brewing machine) through the drive-thru window for preparation in the car! Not surprisingly, the young child spilled the drink and was severely burned as she attempted to prepare the hot chocolate as her father began to drive away.

Foodservice operators may use factory pre-set hot water machines or may use independent foodservice establishment guidelines to make hot cocoa. A visit to our local Starbucks found that it offers hot cocoa made at different temperatures for adults and children. The regular hot cocoa for adults is served at about 160°F (71.1°C), and the children's version is adjusted down to a more moderate 125°F (51.6°C). A trip to the local Dunkin' Donuts offered a 12-ounce cup of hot cocoa, and a temperature check showed the contents to be 172°F (77.7°C). The instant powder cappuccino machines that are found at many convenience stores have factory-set water tank temperatures of 190°F (87.7°C). Upon request, Wilbur Curtis Co. Inc., one of the leading commercial hot beverage machine manufacturers, supplied a temperature reading from one of its instant cappuccino and hot cocoa machines. The company reported that the temperature reading at the spout was 180°F (82.2°C), and when the 12-ounce cup was filled with hot cocoa, it was 175-180°F (79.4-82.2°C). These readings bear the assumption that most people do not add cold milk or other dairy products to the drink because it already contains either steamed milk or dry milk solids.

In terms of the preparation of hot cocoa at home, it is a challenge to find a hot chocolate package for consumers' use that states a specific water temperature. Many instructions offer renditions of the recommendation, "Gradually stir 6 oz. (3/4 cup) hot (not boiling) milk or water into mix," or microwave directions, "Heat 6 oz. (3/4 cup) milk or water on HIGH power 1 minute or until hot (not boiling)." What temperature is a microwave oven's high power for 1 minute? What temperature is hot (not boiling)? What hot cocoa temperature is appropriate for children?

This much we do know: preparation of hot cocoa should be completed and delivered in a securely lidded cup with no further action required by the consumer. This is also in consideration of the fact that the drink is commonly served to children. Further, we suggest the serving temperature should be much lower than that of hot teas and coffees, such as the 125°F (51.6°C) cocoa offered to children at Starbucks. This recommendation is possible because the quality and flavor of hot cocoa are not compromised by lower temperatures (only the non-dairy solids need to be dissolved in hot water), and cooler temperature dairy products are usually included or can be added to the drink. Additionally, as will be explained more fully in the Burn Equation section that follows, the serving size of hot beverages for children should be limited to 5-6 ounces served in an 8-ounce lidded cup.

Too Hot or Not-too Hot?

In a study done by C.P. Borchgrevink, A. M. Susskind, and J.M. Tarras, "Consumer Preferred Hot Beverage Temperatures,"[6] researchers found that a majority of consumers like their coffee to be served very hot—between 176 and 185°F (80-85°C). In a different study, "Hedonic R-Index Measurement of Temperature Preferences for Drinking Black Coffee,"[7] conducted by S. Pipatsattayanuwong, H.S. Lee, and M. O'Mahony, the researchers asked study participants to rank, by order of preference, the temperatures at which to drink black coffee. Nearly seventy-five percent of the participants favored a temperature of 161.8°F (72.1°C); the least preferred temperature (3.1%) was 102.6°F (39.2°C)—the only temperature in the study that was below the skin damage threshold if spilled.

Professor O'Mahony also asked study participants to rank the order of black coffee temperatures that they thought would most likely be found served in a coffee shop. Their rankings were obtained by pouring "a full cup of coffee from each server into a paper cup and immediately judging the temperature. Some judged coffee temperature by feeling the cup with their hands and did not drink the coffee, some judged by swallowing a sip of coffee, while others judged by doing both. More than ninety-nine percent reported that they would not be surprised to be served hot coffee at 167.2°F (75.1°C)—again, temperatures well above skin burn thresholds if spilled.

Drinking Temperature Preferences[7]
Preference for temperatures at which to drink black coffee

Temperature	Percentage of judges who liked this temperature
161.8°F (72.1°C) *Most Preferred*	74.2%
141.7°F (60.9°C)	63.6%
169.8°F (76.5°C)	40.9%
121.6°F (49.8°C)	16.4%
179.8°F (82.1°C)	9.8%
102.5°F (39.2°C) *Least Preferred*	3.1%

Expected Serving Temperatures[7]
Order of temperatures that judges thought would most likely be found for black coffee served in coffee shop

Temperature	Percentage of judges who would not be surprised at having coffee served at this temperature
167.2°F (75.1°C) *Most Expected*	99.1%
144.7°F (62.6°C)	93.0%
177.2°F (80.7°C)	80.3%
186.3°F (85.7°C)	59.6%
123.5°F (50.8°C)	23.9%
103.7°F (39.8°C) *Least Expected*	5.2%

Such studies, as well as consumers' everyday behaviors, confirm that people do expect to be served and to sip their drinks at the customary temperatures used to brew and serve hot coffee. What consumers do not seem aware of and do not seem to expect is that when spilled—not sipped—hot tea or hot coffee can cause second- or third-degree burns.

Most people take small exploratory sips to gauge the temperature of a hot beverage. An exploratory sip is usually 5ml or less. The minute quantity limits the heat energy available for transfer to the skin and a sip is not usually held in the mouth for enough time to cause pain or tissue damage.

Why Doesn't Your Mouth Burn?

Science explains the very particular hot water temperatures required for extracting appealing flavors from tea leaves and ground coffee beans. Science also explains the relatively confounding fact that the mouth does not suffer scald burns when sipping hot soup, hot tea or coffee—but when spilled on the skin—the result can be instant first-, second-, or third-degree burns.

Whether in a commercial establishment or a home kitchen, the temperatures required to brew hot coffee and tea are well above the skin burn threshold. An automatic drip coffeemaker brews at 195°F (90.5°C) or higher, and water from a teakettle comes off the boil near 212°F (100°C). How can it be that we drink at such high temperatures when human skin begins to burn at 130°F (54.4°C)? All hot foods served to the public must be held at or above 130°F (54°C)[8] to comply with the United States Department of Agriculture (USDA) food safety regulations, and even that modest requirement is above the skin burn threshold. Why don't our mouths burn when sipping hot drinks or taking spoonfuls of soup at such high temperatures? How does it follow that other parts of our body suffer third-degree burns in one second at 156°F (68.9°C)? [9]

Professor O'Mahony also examined this curious fact in another study, "Drinking Hot Coffee: Why Doesn't It Burn the Mouth?"[10] His hypothesis follows:

> Coffee served at temperatures recommended by the hospitality and food literature for brewing and holding is above thermal pain and damage thresholds. Yet, consumers do not report pain or damage on drinking coffee at such temperatures. To investigate this discrepancy, the temperature of hot coffee before and during sipping was investigated for 18 subjects. Coffee temperature was continuously monitored by thermocouples in the cup, in the coffee bolus in the oral cavity, and on the surface of the tongue. There was minimal cooling as the coffee entered the mouth from the cup, yet the coffee temperature was still above the threshold for inducing burn damage. It is hypothesized that during drinking, the bolus of hot coffee is not held in the mouth long enough to heat the epithelial surfaces sufficiently to cause pain or tissue damage.

Professor O'Mahony's study concluded:

> That the subjects did not report pain when sipping hot coffee indicates that the hot coffee never contacted the intra-oral epithelial surface long enough to induce pain or tissue damage.
>
> Thus, if coffee is used as intended, namely to be sipped and swallowed, the normal serving temperatures

would not cause burn damage. On the other hand, if coffee at these temperatures were spilled, it could be held in place by clothing long enough to cause burns. Furthermore, coffee at temperatures well above normal serving temperatures also has the potential to produce burn damage.

The mouth's tolerance for higher temperatures was also confirmed in researcher Barry G. Green's study, "Heat Pain Thresholds in the Oral-facial Region."[11] Green stated, "Common experience seems to support the idea that the mouth is relatively insensitive to thermal pain, hot but drinkable coffee and tea are held in insulated containers or in cups with handles to avoid burning the hands, and cooked foods such as baked potatoes are often eaten when too hot to handle. Although oral intake of such foods can be modified to accommodate their high temperatures (e.g., by sipping or eating small portions), one need only dip a finger briefly into a hot beverage to become suspicious of the mouth's sensitivity to potentially harmful temperatures." Further, "All evidence, both sensorineural and psychophysical points to use of the hands, lips, and tongue tip to assess the thermal suitability of potential foods before ingestion."

We take small exploratory sips before we consume larger quantities of hot soups or drinks. Sipping is considered consuming a very small amount of liquid—about a scant teaspoon (~5ml). The primary reason the mouth does not burn when taking sips is that a smaller amount of hot liquid has less heat energy to transfer to surrounding tissues. This relationship between heat transfer and quantity also explains the profound difference between taking a 5ml sip and spilling a 16-ounce cup of hot liquid onto your skin.

This research verifies our collective experience: the mouth can and does tolerate small quantities of hot foods and beverages at temperatures well above the pain and burn damage threshold. Drinking a hot beverage prepared to industry recommendations is safe when sipped as intended.

Thermal Scald Skin Burns
Scald Burn Equation: Temperature + Quantity + Time = Severity

Despite the fact that temperature has not been a contentious issue in terms of customer's expected serving and preferred drinking temperatures, it has been an issue and the focus of most plaintiff claims in hot beverage spill lawsuits. However, three variables play critical roles and contribute to burn severity: temperature, quantity, and time (duration of contact between the burn medium and the skin). Misunderstanding the dynamic interplay of these variables has led to many false assumptions, such as the common claim that the product was defective because it was made excessively hot. It also helps to explain why you can sip very hot coffee safely and yet burn badly when a quantity of the same beverage is spilled onto your skin. The lack of understanding about the interplay of these three variables has led to the erroneous claims that if the hot drink had been properly made consumers would not suffer terrible burns when spilled.

In addition to temperature, quantity is the second important variable in hot liquid spills. Quantity impacts the available heat energy transferred from the hot liquid to a person's cooler temperature skin. Although heat energy and temperature are related to each other, they are different concepts.

Temperature is a measure of how hot or cold a substance is, and temperature does not change with quantity. Heat is the flow of thermal energy transferred from hotter to cooler objects that are in contact. It is thermal energy in transit and does incorporate the quantity of matter involved. Therefore, quantity impacts the available thermal energy and explains the difference when a person safely sips 5 ml of an 185°F hot drink or burns when a 24-ounces of the same temperature beverage contacts his or her room temperature skin. There is a dramatic increase in available heat energy as beverage size increases and accounts for the greater burn risk factors accompanying larger portion spills. For example, in the chart below, Coffee Enterprises calculated and compared the available heat energy measured in British Thermal Units (BTU) for four different cup sizes of room temperature 72°F (22.2°C) coffee. Surprising or not-so, the conclusion shows that there is more than 200 times the amount of available heat energy in a large 24-ounce cup than there is in the 5ml sip.

Coffee Enterprises: Heat Energy by Quantity Comparison

Starting Temperature	Quantity	Available Heat Energy
72°F (22.2°C)	5 ml (sip) = 0.169 fluid ounces = 0.176 ounces = 0.1463 BTU	
72°F (22.2°C)	12 fluid ounce cup = 12.48 ounces =103.74 BTU	
72°F (22.2°C)	16 fluid ounce cup = 16.64 ounces = 138.32 BTU	
72°F (22.2°C)	20 fluid ounce cup = 20.80 ounces = 172.90 BTU	
72°F (22.2°C)	24 fluid ounce cup = 24.96 ounces = 207.48 BTU	

Study assumptions:
1 British Thermal Unit (BTU) of heat energy raises the temperature of 1 pound of water at sea level from 60°F to 61°F
1 gallon of water at 62°F at sea level weighs 8.33 pounds
1 fluid ounce of water (30.26 ml) at 62°F at sea level = 1.04 ounces

Quantity is not only of significance in the burn severity equation, but it is also pertinent to consumers' profound underestimation of hazards when handling hot beverages. It is understandable. Not only have consumers sipped their hot drinks without burning their mouths but it's also likely they've had an inattentive moment or two in their home kitchens. Beads of hot liquid may have spattered onto an arm during stovetop cooking, or a few drips from under the coffee filter may have fallen onto a hand when removing the pot too soon. They probably were startled but quickly responded reflexively, thus limiting both quantity and contact time when they pulled away from the spill, wiped it off, and cooled the area under tap water. They may have experienced some passing discomfort, a brief period of skin redness, or even a small blister that a little home first aid and time healed readily. Again, such momentarily discomfiting experiences have not served well to raise public awareness about how larger quantities of the same hot liquid render notably different and much more injurious results.

The third variable in the scald burn equation is time—the duration of skin contact with the hot liquid. Several factors influence the contact time. Clothing can reduce the temperature of the liquid before it reaches the skin or it can prolong the burn duration. Soft cotton yoga pants, denim blue jeans, or a waterproof windbreaker will obviously impact how quickly a hot liquid is absorbed and how long it is held close to the skin. The longer the contact time, the greater potential for significant burns. Another factor that influences contact time is viscosity—thicker liquids (sauces, cream, honey, oil, butter, soup, or melted cheese) remain on the skin longer, causing more severe burns than hot water at the same temperature and quantity. A study titled "Hot soup! Correlating the Severity of Liquid Scald Burns to Fluid and Biomedical Properties"[12] by researchers from Robert Morris University confirmed that "...more viscous fluids result in more severe burns as the slower flowing thicker fluids remain in contact with the skin for longer."

Contact time is further affected by one's ability to act quickly or reflexively. Under ordinary circumstances, a person who accidentally places a hand on a hot stove burner will recoil and draw his or her hand away at once. These normal withdrawal reflexes are usually measured in milliseconds.[13] Although spilling a hot liquid usually prompts a reflexive withdrawal, one's ability to act on that quick reflex might be delayed in more restrictive circumstances, such as when consuming a hot drink while in a moving vehicle. Consider the two following examples: Person A stands at a convenience store counter and sloshes a sixteen-ounce cup of 165°F (73.8°C) coffee onto his or her arm while picking up the cup; person B spills his or her sixteen-ounce cup of 165°F (73.8°C) cup while seat-belted and driving or riding down the highway. It's likely the person standing in the convenience store will instantly pull back and away as the spilled coffee rolls down and off the skin, and even if the liquid soaked a jacket or shirtsleeve, the fabric could be pulled away within seconds. There also might be ready access to tap water and cool cloths to help stop the burning. The driver, however, will be challenged to act safely and reflexively while seat-belted and maneuvering a car down the highway. When the full cup of coffee spills onto the driver's lap, valuable seconds and minutes are lost as he or she must slow down to pull off the road, stop, unbuckle, and exit the car before removing saturated clothing and tending to the burn. In these two scenarios, the spilled liquids' temperatures might be identical, but the differences in the quantity spilled and the contact time could make for ruthlessly different outcomes.

In addition to the burn equation variables of temperature, time, and quantity, human factors also contribute to the severity of a hot liquid scald burn, such as the burn victim's age, health status, the percentage of surface area involved, and the burn location. Skin thicknesses vary—the elderly, infants, and young children have thinner, more fragile skin. A forearm may have thicker skin than the inner thigh. Most men may have thicker skin than women do. And for individuals with certain health issues, such as diabetes, even a small burn could produce more complex situations and worrying outcomes.

Hot water causes third degree burns...

...in 1 second at 156°F (68.8°C)
...in 2 seconds at 149°F (65.0°C)
...in 5 seconds at 140°F (60.0°C)
...in 15 seconds at 133°F (56.1°C)

Burn Foundation[1]

Thermal Scald Burns

Stella Liebeck's lawsuit[14] was scoffed at, in part, because the public underestimated the impact of second- and third-degree burns. They also appear relatively unaware that there are many other spill lawsuits with plaintiffs that have suffered similar burns. The next section will briefly describe the impact and damage of thermal scald burns. Increased awareness of the burns and skin damage possible from hot beverage spills might encourage greater caution when handling hot drinks on the go. Increased awareness might also serve to boost industry-wide efforts to improve cup and lid safety, issue more effective warnings, and to train staff in the best practices to handle hot drinks securely.

Skin Damage

Skin is the body's natural barrier to guard against infection and organ injury; it regulates body temperature, prevents fluid loss, and is a vital sensory organ. Skin burns are classified by the extent of the burned area (the amount of body surface damaged) and the depth of tissue damage through the three layers of skin cells and tissue: first-degree (*superficial*) burns, second-degree (*superficial or deep partial-thickness*) burns, and third-degree (*full-thickness*) burns.

The University of Wisconsin Burn Center describes the three degrees of burns thus:

> First-degree burns are the least severe type of burn because only the outer layer of the skin is damaged. As with sunburn, the skin turns red and may feel warm and painful. However, there are no blisters or open areas. First-degree burns can heal on their own without medical treatment. Recommended treatment methods are soaking the affected area in cool water (not ice water) for five minutes and

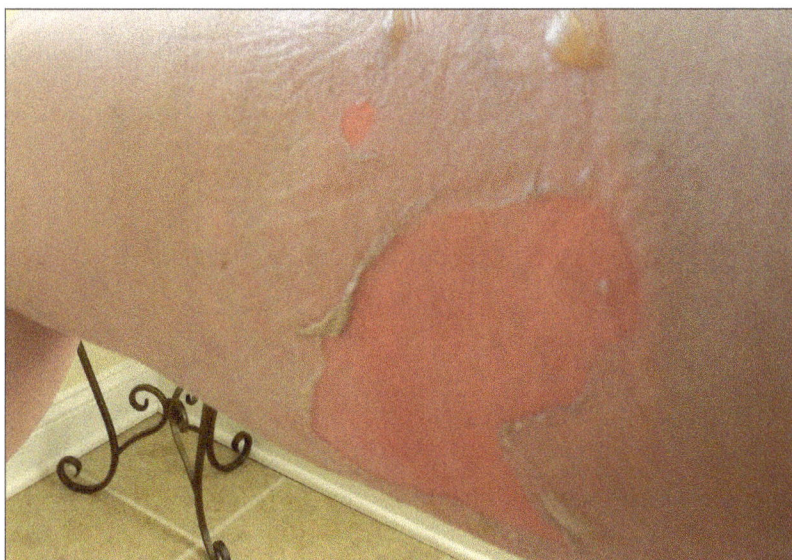

Second-degree burns produce red, blistered, peeling skin and pain!

covering with a clean bandage. Over-the-counter pain medications such as Ibuprofen may be used to relieve pain.

Second-degree burns are more severe since they damage part of the inner layer of the skin as well as its outer layer. The burned area turns pink or red, is very moist and develops blisters. As with first-degree burns, this type of burn can usually heal on its own if it is not very deep. However, if the burn is deep, the healing skin will be more fragile and is likely to reopen. Skin grafting may be necessary for deep second-degree burns if (1) the burn takes a long time to heal, (2) severe scarring occurs, and/or (3) the burn reopens.

Third-degree burns are the most severe type since they destroy both the outer and inner layers of the skin. The burn may appear white or leathery, and may not be painful. (Third-degree burns can sometimes destroy the pain-sensing cells in the skin.) Very small third-degree burns may heal on their own, but this process takes a very long time. Any third-degree burn larger than a fifty-cent piece must be grafted, or it will not heal. [15]

Although minor burns can be treated at home, even small first-degree superficial burns may cause complications if not given the appropriate care. People whose skin has burned are particularly vulnerable to infection. Additionally, in widespread or deeper burns, fluid loss can lead to dehydration and medical shock if not promptly treated with intravenous (IV) fluids.[16] Deep or extensive burns may also require specialized burn treatment care to remove dead tissue (a process called debridement) and skin grafts. When skin grafts are necessary, artificial skin or a piece of the burn victim's (or donor's) skin is taken from another part of the body to be surgically attached.

When large or more sensitive areas are affected by any burn, the severity and treatment of the injury become more complex. Dr. David Leitner, a plastic surgeon at the University of Vermont Medical Center, offers a cringe-worthy and cautionary example for consumers that drink hot beverages while in moving vehicles: "Hot liquid spills on the lap and groin area can create circumstances that may affect urination, the ability to have sexual intercourse, and a woman's ability to have a vaginal birth." Unfortunately, this warning is not hyperbolic or hypothetical; there have been several lawsuits where plaintiffs have spilled a large cup of hot coffee or tea in their laps while in vehicles and have suffered such life-altering burns.

Although every individual situation is unique, many burns leave scars. Superficial burns may leave a pink or white discoloration that fades with time. Children may overproduce scar tissue, and superficial burns may be visible for many years before fading. If burns are deep, the scars may be permanent and disfiguring. Scar tissue may also limit the mobility and functioning of the area. Additionally, in full-thickness burns, sweat glands may not regenerate, and skin pigmentation may disappear.

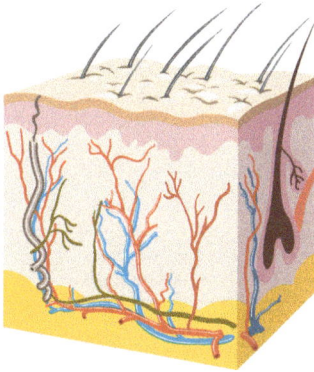

NORMAL SKIN

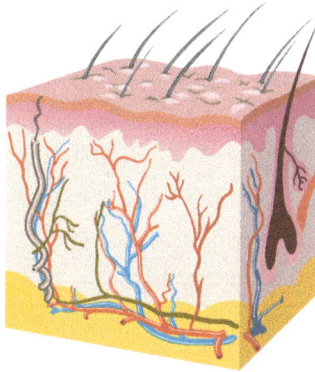

FIRST DEGREE BURN

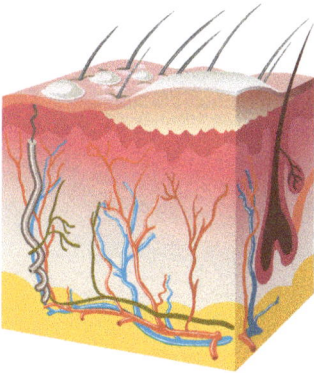

SECOND DEGREE BURN

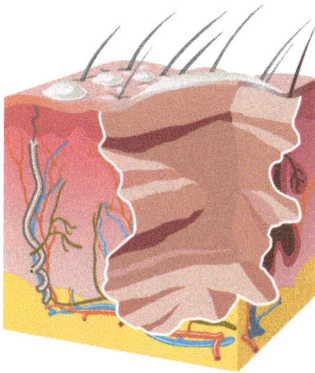

THIRD DEGREE BURN

Burn Depth, Skin Damage, Pain, Healing, and Scars[15]

Full/Partial Burn	Degree	Depth of Damage
Partial Thickness Burns	First Degree	Epidermis
Partial Thickness Burns	Second Degree *Superficial*	Epidermis and top of dermis
	Second Degree *Deep*	Epidermis and deep into dermis
Full Thickness Burns	Third Degree	Epidermis and all of dermis

Medical or Psychological Shock

Scald burns can be devastating. Other reactions to a second- or third-degree burn can be medical or psychological shock. Medical shock is a life-threatening emergency that requires immediate treatment as symptoms can worsen rapidly. Medical shock may result from trauma, severe burns, blood or fluid loss, infection, or other causes. In medical shock, the person's organs do not receive enough blood or oxygen. If untreated, this can lead to permanent organ damage or even death.[16]

A scald burn victim may suffer from medical shock and/or psychological shock, a layperson's term for what is more accurately called *acute stress disorder*. This response sometimes appears soon after and as the result of experiencing a traumatic event. It can be part of the burn victim's reaction to suffering significant wounds and pain, scarring or disfigurement, and/or the loss of mobility and function in an injured body part. Acute stress disorder typically causes intense feelings of fear, sadness, anxiety, and dissociative symptoms [being numb, less aware of surroundings, and a dissociative sense of self]. Dissociative symptoms distinguish acute stress disorder from

Pain	Heal Time	Scars?
Painful	5-7 days	No
Extreme pain and hypersensitivity	7-15 days	No
Usually painful	15-30 days	May leave hypertrophic/ thick scars
Usually not painful; nerve endings have been destroyed	REQUIRES SKIN GRAFTING	

post-traumatic stress disorder (PTSD). However, if left unresolved, acute stress disorder can progress and evolve into PTSD.[17]

People who have suffered deep second- and third-degree burns may have had their lives upended. They may have endured repeated hospitalizations, suffered great pain, and have been permanently disfigured by skin grafts and scars. A significant burn injury may also have imposed a loss of function that compromised the person's ability to work or to perform routine activities of daily living independently. The victim may require an extended period for rehabilitation with multiple support services. Subsequently, the medical issues tumble into genuine psycho-social problems, such as the loss of independence, work, income, as well as a diminished ability to participate in meaningful activities.

Beverage Temperature & Burn Threshold Summary

Temperature in °F	100	105	110	115	120	125	130	135	140	145
Reference temperatures	Hot tub water 100-104°F				Home hot water heater 120°F					
Pain & burn threshholds		Skin pain threshhold 107.6-109.4°F					Burn damage threshhold 130-135°F			
3rd degree burns acquired at x temp.							3rd degree burns @ 133°F in 15 sec		3rd degree burns @ 140°F in 5 sec	
Consumer preferences for serving temperatures (O'Mahoney Studies)										
Industry standards for brewing and holding hot coffee										
Espresso/ steamed milk drinks										
Tea steeping range										

Above skin pain threshhold
Below burn damage threshhold

Above skin pain threshhold
Above burn damage threshhold

150	155	160	165	170	175	180	185	190	195	200	210	215	220	225	230

Boiling water 212°F

Above skin pain and burn damage threshholds

3rd degree burns @ 149°F in 2 sec

3rd degree burns @ 150°F within 1 second

Most preferred sipping temp. 161.8°F

Most expected serving temp 167.2°F

Average temp (black) at first sip 168°F

Recommended serving temp 165-175°F

Holding temp range 175-185°F

Home brewer holding range (2 min after brew cycle completion) 175-205°F

Brew temp range (comm. & home) 195-205°F

Steamed milk temp. range

Espresso brewing range

Steam

Tea steep range 208-212°F

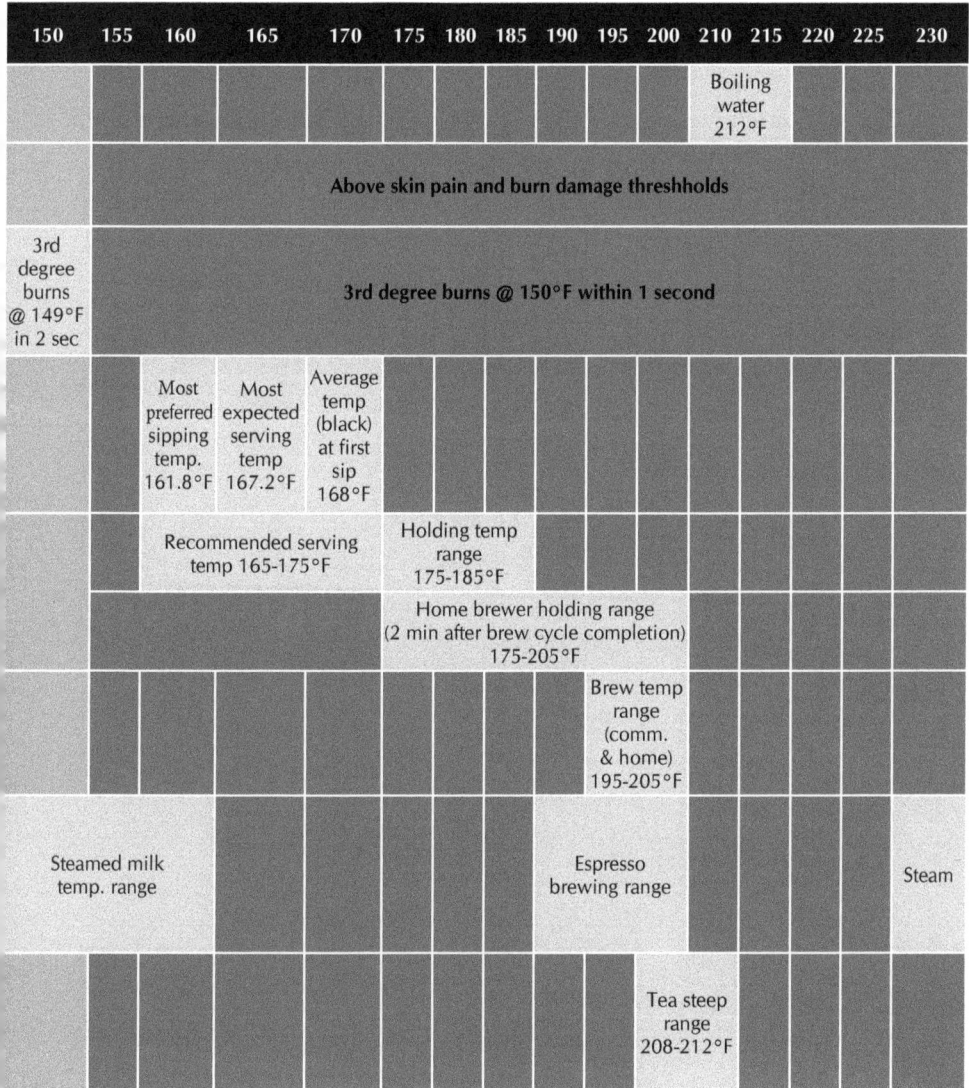

■ Above skin pain threshhold
■ Above burn damage threshhold

115

Avoiding Burns
Lower the Temperature or Prevent the Spill?

The hot beverage industry has best practice recommendations (Chapter 4) for brewing and holding temperatures for hot beverages, but it cannot offer such advice for consumer drinking temperatures. Consumers' preferred drinking temperatures are above skin burn thresholds and can vary by more than twenty degrees. In some hot beverage spill litigation, plaintiffs have called upon physicians and other burn experts to testify on the burn hazards of hot beverage spills and to call for lower hot beverage serving temperatures. However, these recommendations often are not grounded in the science and recommendations for extracting flavors from tea leaves and coffee beans. Lowering the temperature for serving children cocoa is the only exception. Lowering serving temperatures for hot coffees and teas to be closer to skin burn thresholds would compromise flavor and quality, be unwelcome by consumers and purveyors, and would be an impractical gesture: "breakdown of flavor will speed up if there is any fluctuation of temperature. Beverage coffee should never be allowed to cool and then be reheated."[18]

How would a lower standard set-point for serving tea or coffee accommodate a range of consumer preferences that run from black and very hot to tea or coffee with lots of milk or cream? People's tolerance and preference for eating hot food or drinking hot beverages above the skin's threshold for pain and damage are well documented. Evidence shows that consumers like their beverages served hot, take exploratory sips, and drink at their preferred temperatures.[4] Thus, serving coffee in the hotter range of recommended holding temperatures of 175-185°F (79.4-85°C) maintains optimal flavor profiles and is more time- and energy-efficient than is serving coffee at or below skin damage thresholds. This way, coffee is served so that most consumers who like their coffee at 160-175°F (71.1-79.4°C) will be content, and those who prefer their coffee cooler can wait before drinking the beverage or request the addition of an ice cube or cold milk/cream. Professor O'Mahony's studies showed that people are accustomed to waiting at least thirty seconds before they take their first exploratory sips. Further, coffee cools through each stage of processing before reaching the consumer, and it continues to cool while in the consumer's possession. Lowering serving temperatures nearer to or below skin burn thresholds would just result in many refunds or requests for coffee to be reheated to warmer temperatures or replaced.

In sum, to lower hot beverage serving temperatures below the skin burn threshold would meet with public failure because it would compromise beverage quality; secondly, it would be logistically burdensome and impractical for foodservice operators to institute. However well-intentioned any lowered temperature suggestions may be, they are nonetheless misplaced safety efforts that would waste energy, consumers' and baristas' time, and defeat retailers' efforts to meet the public's demand for quality products with swift, efficient service.

Spilling a hot beverage is unquestionably more dangerous than sipping it is. A reasonable degree of care must be taken with any food or drink that can cause harm when mishandled—whether it is hot soup, eggs, meat, dairy, sushi, alcohol, or hot beverages. Handling knives take care; operating a deli slicer takes attentiveness; driving a vehicle takes vigilance and concentration. Hot beverage spills are an atypical, accidental event. Instead of tampering with and compromising well-researched industry recommendations for brewing and holding temperatures in response to occasional spill accidents, it is time to shift focus and gain traction in exploring more appropriate and effective measures to prevent hot beverage spills altogether.

Temperature Loss Over Time
Coffee Enterprises Study

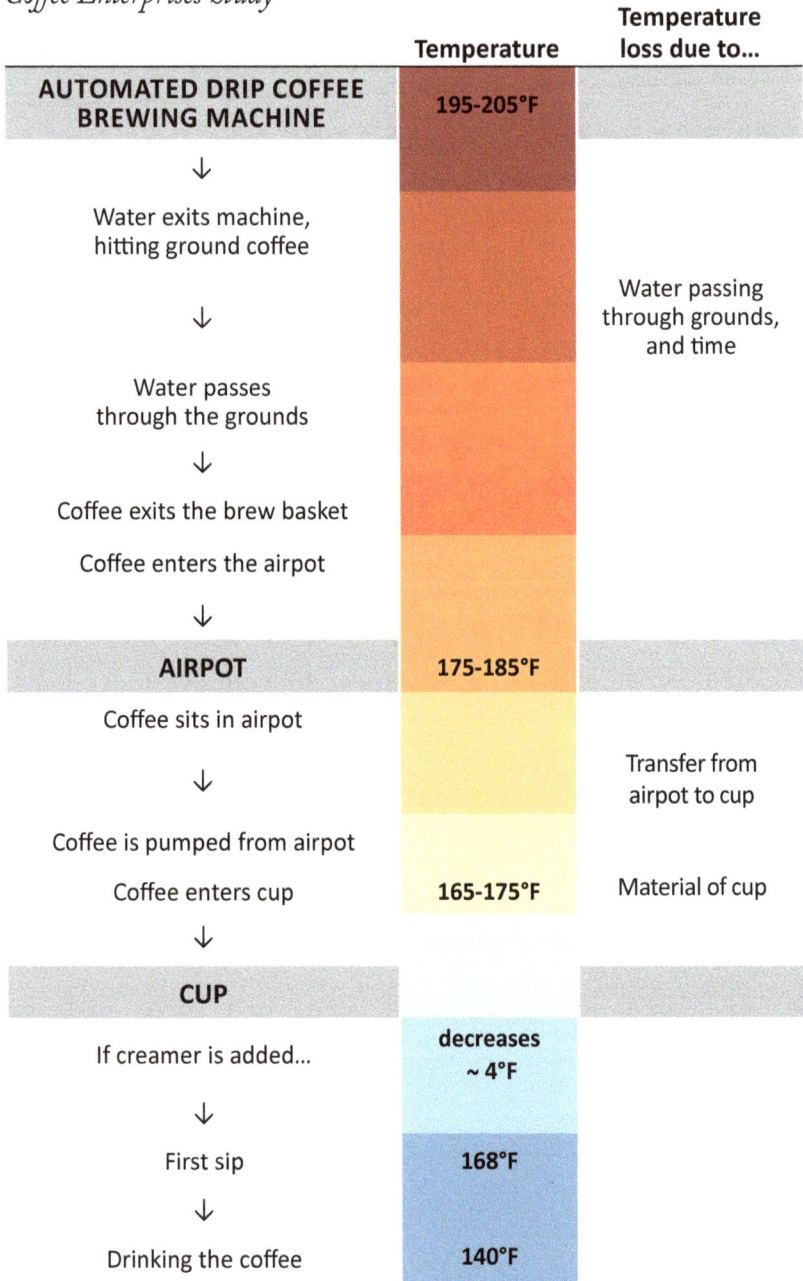

	Temperature	Temperature loss due to...
AUTOMATED DRIP COFFEE BREWING MACHINE	195-205°F	
↓		
Water exits machine, hitting ground coffee		
↓		Water passing through grounds, and time
Water passes through the grounds		
↓		
Coffee exits the brew basket		
Coffee enters the airpot		
↓		
AIRPOT	175-185°F	
Coffee sits in airpot		
↓		Transfer from airpot to cup
Coffee is pumped from airpot		
Coffee enters cup	165-175°F	Material of cup
↓		
CUP		
If creamer is added...	**decreases ~ 4°F**	
↓		
First sip	**168°F**	
↓		
Drinking the coffee	**140°F**	

Citations

1. "Take The Scald Test" Burn Foundation, http://www. burnfoundation.org/assets/asset_1063.pdf (accessed December 04, 2017).

2. *Coffee Brewing Workshop Manual*: Publication 54. (New York:Coffee Brewing Center of the Pan-American Coffee Bureau, Revised 1974).

3. Ted R. Lingle, *The Coffee Brewing Handbook: A Systematic Guide to Coffee Preparation* (Long Beach, CA: Specialty Coffee Association of American, 1996)

4. Recommendations for the Preparation of Iced and Hot Tea by the Tea Association of the USA, Inc. published in cooperation with the National Restaurant Association, 2011

5. SCAA Golden Cup Standard, Published by the Specialty Coffee Association of America , Revised: December 2015

6. Borchgrevink, C. P., Susskind, A. M., & Tarras, J. M. (1999). "Consumer Preferred Hot Beverage Temperatures." *Food Quality and Preference, 10*(2), 117-121.

7. Pipatsattayanuwong, S., H.S. Lee, and M. O'Mahony. "Hedonic R-Index Measurement of Temperature Preferences for Drinking Black Coffee." *Journal of Sensory Studies* 16.5 (2001):517-36.

8. https://www.fsis.usda.gov/wps/wcm/connect/fsis-content/internet/ main/topics/regulations/advisory-committees/nacmcf-reports/ nacmcf-report-hot-holding-2002 accessed 3/8/2018

9. Burn Foundation "Safety Facts on Scald Burns" http://www. burnfoundation.org/programs/resource.cfm?c=1&a=3

10. Lee, H.-S., Carstens, E. and O'Mahony, M. "Drinking Hot Coffee: Why Doesn't it Burn the Mouth?" *Journal of Sensory Studies*, (2003), 18: 19–32.

11. Barry G. Green, "Heat Pain Thresholds in the Oral- facial Region," *Perception & Psychophysics* 1985, 38 (2), 110-114

12. Loller, Buxton, and Kerzmann "Hot soup! Correlating the severity of liquid scald burns to fluid and biomedical properties" *Burns Journal*, abstract http://www.burnsjournal.com/article/ S0305-4179(15)00326-5/fulltext https://www.researchgate.net/ publication/291517593

13. Pierrot-Deseilligny, Emmanuel, David C. Burke, and David H.

Burke. "Withdrawal Reflexes." The Circuitry of the Human Spinal Cord: Spinal and Corticospinal Mechanisms of Movement. 2nd ed. N.P.: Cambridge University Press, 2005

14. *Liebeck v. McDonald's Restaurants, P.T.S., Inc.,* No. CV-93-02419, 1995 WL 360309, Second Judicial District Court of New Mexico, Bernalillo County, August 14, 1994.

15. Burn Center Frequently Asked Questions | Uw Health, https://www.uwhealth.org/burn-center/burn-center-frequently-asked-questions/2961 (accessed January 13, 2018).

16. Shock: First Aid - Mayo Clinic, http://www.mayoclinic.org/first-aid/first-aid-shock/basics/ART-20056620 (accessed December 04, 2017).

17. DoveMed, "Psychological Shock" Web: http://www.dovemed.com/article-synonyms/psychological-shock/ July 2017

18. *Coffee Brewing Workshop Manual*: Publication 54. (New York: Coffee Brewing Center of the Pan-American Coffee Bureau, Revised

CHAPTER FOUR

Best Practices

Recommendations for Commercial Operations

With Spencer Turer, Vice-President, Coffee Enterprises

Coffee, tea, and cocoa are familiar beverages. They are prepared and consumed at home and purchased while away from home. These are beverages that are part of our daily lives and statistics have confirmed our enduring affinity for these hot and delicious drinks. Preparation, holding, and serving hot beverages for quality and consistency is more challenging and complicated in commercial operations than for the home consumer. The coffee and tea industries have met that challenge and flourished as a result of their untiring quest to produce high-quality beverages that consumers purchase and enjoy.

Research from the National Coffee Association Drinking Trends (NCDT) reports:

"Since 1954 the National Coffee Association USA has conducted a drinking survey of American adults, providing statistical information on coffee consumer drinking patterns.

In 2017 the research listed 62% past day penetration for coffee consumption and 50% for tea. 40% of the people who drank coffee yesterday, drank coffee prepared out-of-home. The growth of the out-of-home market has increased from 9% to 18% since 2012 for café/coffee/donut shop, for quick service restaurants the growth has increased from 4% to 6% since 2012."[1]

There are many distinct preparation methods for hot beverages that differ from consumer to consumer and vary by strength, temperature, drinking vessel, time of day, condiments, etc. Typically, through trial and error testing, we tweak the recipe and beverage preparation using our home equipment. Over time, the repetitive, familiar preparation becomes our unique recipe and ritual, which in turn, builds precision, quality control, and consistency. However,

Although there are many consumer choices for home coffee brewers,
the range of brewing temperatures do not tend to vary by much.

there are great and contrasting differences when food and beverage
preparation transitions from self-preparation at home to products
made by others and purchased in the marketplace.

Chefs and restaurateurs will attest to the challenges of pleasing
everyone with a single recipe or production technique. As
consumers become more sophisticated, and as access to profes-
sional-level training is readily available online or through classes at
local specialty food stores, foodservice establishments must contin-
ually strive to exceed consumer expectations for quality, value, and
consistency—every day.

The days of serving only brewed regular and decaf coffee, teabags
with a pot of hot water, and mixing cocoa powder with hot water
while seated at restaurant tables were simpler times. Take-away

On the left is a coffee brewer made for home use and at right are brewers made for commercial use. Although they may vary by maker, size, and style, the brewing temperatures are similar and relatively standard.

service and drive-thru lanes changed the dynamics of serving hot beverages; the popularity of specialty coffees and teas increased the complexity of menu offerings and drink preparations to meet the level of other gourmet and culinary products.

As understood by chefs and foodservice establishments, food items may be returned for additional cooking or heating whenever requested by the consumer. This is inconvenient for both the consumer and the foodservice operator because it disrupts the flow of service and delays fast-service, take-away orders and when dining with companions. In the case of hot beverages, there is little to no option for increasing the beverage temperature while maintaining the quality after it is prepared, however, the temperature may be easily cooled by simply waiting to consume it. Therefore, the beverages are best when served hot.

The information presented in this chapter will identify both best practices and industry standards for the preparation, holding, and serving of hot beverages. Also, we will provide our opinions for the creation of new best practices and standards to be utilized by the foodservice industry.

Best Practices and Standardization

Best practices are not requirements, but are published methods, processes, or techniques that are regarded by professionals as superior. Best practices for various coffee brewing and extraction processes are detailed and ubiquitous within coffee training programs. The Specialty Coffee Association's "Golden Cup Standard"[2] defines the ideal balance of extraction (soluble yield) and strength (soluble concentration) for drip-brewed coffee and includes variations for the American and European marketplaces. Although there are no mandated industry standards for brewing hot beverages, there are recognized best practices within companies, for market regions, and for industry-wide professional development programs. These are well-researched and detailed recipes, procedures, and protocols.

Standards are created by a recognized authority with established specifications, requirements, methods of measurement, and protocols. There are voluntary standards, consensus standards, and mandatory standards.

Voluntary standards

Voluntary standards are standards generally established by private-sector bodies and that are available for use by any person or organization, private or government. The term includes what are commonly referred to as "industry standards" as well as "consensus standards." A voluntary standard may become mandatory as a result of its use, reference, or adoption by a regulatory authority, or when invoked in contracts, purchase orders, or other commercial instruments.[3]

For example, professional development courses by coffee trade associations and organizations are voluntary standards as part of the educational curriculum.

Consensus standards

Consensus standards are standards developed through the cooperation of all parties who have an interest in participating in the development and/or use of the standards. Consensus requires that all views and objections be considered and that an effort be made toward their resolution. Consensus implies more than the concept of a simple majority but not necessarily unanimity.[3]

For example, coffee and tea competitions for roasting, beverage preparation, and beverage quality, etc. are consensus standards as the basis for judging criteria.

Mandatory standards

A mandatory standard is a standard that requires compliance because of a government statute or regulation, an organization's internal policy, or contractual requirement. Failure to comply with a mandatory standard usually carries a sanction, such as civil or criminal penalties, or loss of employment.[3]

For example, coffee and tea companies follow mandatory standards for Good Manufacturing Practices, HACCP, and FSMA programs. OSHA, FDA, and Health Department regulations are further examples of mandatory standards. Product specifications and preparation recipes are examples of internal company mandatory standards, but not mandatory industry standards.

Hot Beverage Preparations

Tea Brewing Instructions

Tea has been prepared and consumed for centuries and is a favorite beverage around the world. Leaves and buds from the *camellia sinensis* plant are used to make authentic tea beverages. The manner of processing the leaves and buds harvested from the tea gardens will determine the type of tea it becomes. Beverages made from other botanicals are often called tisanes, herbal infusions, or herbal teas. Fortunately, for the purposes of hot beverage preparations, tea and tisanes are prepared very similarly.

This cup of hot tea without a lid is a big no-go! All hot beverages served to-go should be presented to the customer fully prepared with a secure lid.

There are six basic stages of the manufacturing process that produce the six basic tea types—all from the *camellia sinensis* plant. Plucking, withering, rolling and shaping, oxidation, firing, and sorting are the six basic manufacturing processes used to produce different types of teas. White, green, yellow, oolong, black, and pu'erh teas are all prepared using different manufacturing processes from the leaves and buds of the *camellia sinensis* plant.

According to the Tea Association of the U.S.A., interest in hot tea has been growing steadily over the past several years (particularly among millennials), as consumers learn of health benefits of various teas.

As with coffee, three of the essential elements for brewing a good cup of tea are water quality, water temperature (extraction), and steeping (infusion) time. The brewing and steeping process for hot teas involves immersion of loose tea leaves or a teabag in hot water that has been heated to a specific temperature.

Each of the six tea types has different brewing directions, which are determined to bring out the most pleasing and appealing flavors in each beverage. The differences in water temperature are due to the differences in leaf size and processing. The chart below is from the Tea Association of the U.S.A. best practices and standard operating procedures for tea-brewing parameters:

Tea Category	Water Temperature	Steep Time
White	160°F (71°C)	2 minutes
Yellow	160°F (71°C)	2 minutes
Chinese Green	175°F (79°C)	2.5 minutes
Japanese Green	160°F (71°C)	1.5 minutes
Oolong	195°F (90°C)	3.5 minutes
Black	205°F (96°C)	5 minutes
Pu-erh	210°F (99°C)	5 minutes
Tisanes	205°F (96°C)	5 minutes

Instructions:
- Begin with clean equipment.
- Water used for brewing tea should be freshly drawn and heated to the precise temperature. Water that is stale or not at the correct temperature will have a marked effect on the quality of tea beverages. Water should have a pH as close to 7 as possible and contain no impurities and have no odors or recognized taste.
- Warm the teacups and teapots with hot water for several minutes before preparing the beverages. Discard the water before brewing the tea.
- Measure 3g loose leaf tea per 236ml (8oz) water into the teapot.
- Fill the teapot with freshly heated water at the precise temperature, covering with a lid once filled.
- Start a timer as soon as the pots have been filled.
- When the time is up, strain the tea beverage without shaking or pressing leaves, working quickly and consistently to ensure an even flavor extraction.
- Serve immediately and enjoy!

The steeping time may be altered based on the size and cut of the tea leaves. Smaller tea leaves and finer particle sizes will extract flavors during steeping faster than larger teas leaves and coarser particle sizes.

For highest quality, best practices for tea beverages are that tea should be prepared and served to order and not held for any significant amount of time.

In foodservice settings, tea is most often prepared by drawing water from the hot water dispenser of a commercial coffee brewer, a specialized water heater, or by boiling water in a teakettle. Foodservice operations often prioritize speed of service and efficiency and use teabags or tea sachets with a single temperature hot water source. The teabag is placed in the cup, hot water is added, and the cup is immediately handed to the customer; or, the teabag may be handed separately for the customer to prepare the beverage themselves. In both situations, there is little, if any, hold time. It is rare for the person serving the tea beverage to alert or remind the consumer of the standard tea steeping time because the consumer is usually experienced with hot tea preparation and able to determine the ideal steeping time to suit his or her individual flavor preference.

The temperatures at which hot tea is consumed are as uniquely individual as are consumer preferred drinking temperatures for hot coffee. Black tea, like coffee, is often modified with dairy products, sweeteners, or perhaps a squeeze of lemon. Each modifier can affect the cooling of the beverage. Other tea categories are often consumed without any flavor modifiers; thus, the cooling process for consumption is based on the serving temperature and the heat retention of the cup or mug. In brief trials done at Coffee Enterprises, a 20-oz. lidded paper cup of tea served at approximately 195°F (90.5°C) lost an average of 1.6°F per minute in the first 10 minutes.

Coffee Brewing Instructions

There are many chemical and physical reactions that occur between coffee and water to create the extraction process. Salts and acids usually dissolve by ionic dissolution, while caffeine dissolves molecularly. Insoluble and large soluble coffee compounds are extracted by hydrolysis reactions. Solutes in concentration go through a diffusion process called osmosis.

Soluble solids will be extracted from coffee in a variety of ways all occurring at the same time. Factors that affect the extraction are water temperature, brew time, grind particle size, and depth of coffee grinds in the brew basket.

Compounds that are soluble in water are dissolved into the coffee beverage. Water heated to between 195-205°F (90.5-96.1°C) is required to accelerate the chemical reactions and increase the solubility of various compounds. Thus, producing a beverage with intoxicating aromas and delicious tastes are extracted from the coffee grounds. It is a relatively precise set of conditions: if water is too cool, not enough flavor will extract; if water is too hot, the grounds burn and produce an astringent, bitter brew.

The aroma and taste of the hot coffee beverage are developed by the released brew colloids (micro-particles of oil and soluble material from the roasted coffee that are suspended in the liquid). The brew colloids provide the body (mouthfeel) and contribute to aroma and taste. When these solids and compounds are extracted from the coffee grounds at the right water temperature and volume (water-to-grounds ratio), the results are flavorful.

Extensive studies reflect and confirm these brewing temperatures—lower temperatures create thin, under-extracted coffee, and higher water temperatures create astringent, bitter or sour, and over-extracted coffee beverages. Because water temperature has such significant impact on beverage profile and quality, this brewing temperature range has become an industry standard for both commercial and consumer coffee-brewing machines.

Much has been published about coffee brewing. Coffee Enterprises recognizes the expertise of the Specialty Coffee Association (SCA) for brewing topics and industry best practices. The educational curriculum from the SCA as well as the Golden Cup Brewing Standard is derived from coffee quality research led by Professor E. Lockhart from the Massachusetts Institute of Technology in the 1950s.[4] National Coffee Association USA commissioned a research study to determine how to define brewed coffee quality and hired Dr. Lockhart, a food technologist, to lead the research.

This research led to the creation of the Coffee Brewing Control Chart that is used to identify the ideal balance of coffee strength and soluble extraction relative to the coffee dosage and water quantity. The research coordinated both chemical analysis for beverage production with consumer preferences. Other information pertinent to brewing quality coffee was detailed in the study including equipment cleanliness, water quality, water temperature, coffee particle size, and brewing times.

The Coffee Brewing Institute, formed in 1952, created the Golden Cup Award Program which was developed to promote proper coffee brewing for restaurants using the research from Dr. Lockhart. In 1996 the Specialty Coffee Association* (then the Specialty Coffee Association of America) published *the Coffee Brewing Handbook*, written by Ted Lingle, who was executive director of the association.[5] The standards for brewing a quality coffee beverage were from the original work completed by Dr. Lockhart. In 2015 the Specialty Coffee Association's Technical Standards Committee published the SCAA Golden Cup Standard document, to reinforce the importance of brewing standards for beverage quality throughout the specialty coffee industry.

The 195°F to 205°F (90.5°-96.1°C) brewing temperature range standard was established by the Coffee Brewing Center of the Pan-American Coffee Bureau through Dr. Lockhart's research. During sensory analyses, the coffee beverage was determined to have the most pleasing balance of acidity, body, bitterness, and astringency in this temperature range. All four components of coffee's taste increased in intensity with an increase in the brew temperature. Although acidity and body are considered desirable traits, bitterness and astringency are not. Acidity in coffee is regarded as the taste perception of the intrinsic organic acids, for example, citric (citrus fruits: lemon, orange, grapefruit), acetic (white vinegar), malic (apple and pear), quinic (astringent-sour), phosphoric (tangy-sour), tartaric (grape/winy), and lactic acids (sour milk, molasses), and not as pH, which is used to measure the acidity or basicity of a aqueous solution. Bitterness refers to a sharp, unpleasant taste that lacks sweetness and is often chemical-like. Astringency is described as a tannic taste or one that produces a dry, puckering mouthfeel. Temperatures higher than 205°F (96.1°C) resulted in astringent and bitter flavors which are undesirable and temperatures lower than 195°F (90.5°C) resulted in less than optimal extraction producing a thin and weak beverage. Chemical analyses of coffee brewed at different temperatures confirm the sensory findings: there are significant differences in the chemical composition of coffee brewed at different temperatures.[5]

Note: As of January 2017, the Specialty Coffee Association of America, established in 1982, and the Specialty Coffee Association of Europe, established in 1998, have officially become one organization. The unified organization is known as the Specialty Coffee Association (SCA) www.sca.coffee

SCAA Golden Cup Standard[2]

Coffee shall exhibit a brew strength, measured in Total Dissolved Solids, of 11.5 to 13.5 grams per liter, corresponding to 1.15 to 1.35 percent on the SCAA Brewing Control Chart, resulting from a soluble extraction yield of 18 to 22 percent.

BREWING BEST PRACTICES – *to achieve the standard*

Coffee-to-Water Ratio: To achieve the Golden Cup Standard, identified as the SCA optimum for strength and extraction in the United States a ratio of 1:17 is recommended, 1-part coffee to 17 parts water. (55 g/L). The SCA ideal for Europe is 1:16, 1-part coffee to 16 parts water (60 g/L).

Strength – Soluble Concentration from Specialty Coffee Association of America: 1.15%-1.35% (1150-1350 ppm)

Strength – Soluble Concentration from Specialty Coffee Association of Europe (SCAE): 1.2%-1.45% (1200-1450 ppm)

Strength – Soluble Concentration from European Coffee Brewing Center (ECBC): 1.30%-1.55% (1300-1550 ppm)

Extraction – Soluble Yield from all three groups is consistent at 18%-22%

Coffee Preparation Temperature: To achieve the Golden Cup Standard, water temperature, at the point of contact with the coffee, is recommended to fall between 200°F ± 5°(93.0°C ± 3°).

EXPLANATION OF STANDARD

Measurable elements:
- Water: valid when brewing water meets SCA water quality standard
- Grind/particle size distribution: matches the time of coffee-to-water contact

Equipment/brewing device:
- Time of coffee-to-water contact: 1-4 minutes (fine), 4-6 minutes (drip), 6-8 minutes (coarse)
- Temperature: 200°F ± 5°(93.0°C ± 3°)
- Turbulence (mixing action of water flowing through and around the coffee particles to achieve a uniform extraction of soluble material)
- Filter media (least affect to brew flavor, body, time of contact and sediment less than 75 milligrams per 100 milliliters).

Five Key Elements for Beverage Quality

For foodservice operators and coffee cafés, quality control should not end with the evaluation of purchases. Beverage reputations are contingent on the quality and consistency of the beverages prepared and served, requiring coffee, tea, and cocoa quality to be managed until it is finally enjoyed by the consumer. Ensuring brewing and serving standards are met includes great attention to details, having the right tools available and knowing how to use those tools, and most importantly, the motivation to provide great beverages in a safe manner.

Green coffee sourcing, blending, roasting, grinding, and packing are all internal process controls designed to maximize coffee flavor. Controlling the foodservice environment to maintain the beverage flavor that operators and business owners work so hard to purchase is no easy task.

The true measure of any beverage program is the quality: how does it taste? Branding, promotion, and merchandising will capture the first sale, but only quality will keep your customers returning time after time.

Great care must be taken to ensure the intrinsic quality of the beverage, from farm-to-cup, is maintained by the brewing process and by the person preparing the beverage.

1. CLEANLINESS: The simplest way to improve and maintain beverage quality is to clean the brewing equipment before brewing. Natural oils and fine particles coat the equipment, and if not cleaned properly may become rancid and cause burnt, bitter, and sour tastes to transfer from dirty equipment into a new brew. You don't cook food in dirty pots—don't make coffee in dirty brewers!

2. FRESHNESS: Roasted coffee is highly perishable and must be treated with care. Tea and powdered cocoa are more stable; however, care must still be taken to prevent it from becoming stale or contaminated in storage. Whole bean coffee can stay at optimum freshness for up to two weeks, but ground coffee will only remain at optimal freshness for less than one hour in an ambient environment. Store all beverage ingredients in a cool, dry place away from light, heat, moisture, and strong odors to maintain quality. Stale ingredients will cause formation of off-flavors, lose aromatics, sweetness, pleasing taste, and body. Over time stale ingredients also will develop malt, paper, and cereal characteristics, as well as rancidity.

3. GRIND: Grinding coffee, pulverizing cocoa, and rolling, cutting, or shaping tea reduces the particle size, increases the surface area, and plays a primary role in developing aromatics and taste in the beverage through extraction. The level of grind must match the brewing method and is predicated on the length of the brewing cycle. Finer particle sizes brew at a faster rate than coarser particle sizes, which brew at a slower rate. For example, espresso at an extra-fine grind brews quicker than French press coffee at a coarse grind, and teabags brew faster than loose leaf tea. Grind coffee immediately before brewing to retain aromatics, sweetness, and freshness.

4. WATER: as the finished brew comprises 98%-99% water, it is critical for the water to be neutral, at the proper temperature, and the right volume. Optimal water quality for brewing beverages is free from any unpleasant aromas or tastes. The Specialty Coffee Association water quality standard for brewing coffee specifies that water should be clear and free of odors and flavors. Also, have a measurable chlorine, a target TDS (Total Dissolved Solids) 150 mg/L (ppm) with an acceptable range 75-250 mg/L, a total alkalinity target 40 mg/L, Calcium hardness target 68 mg/L with an acceptable range between 17 mg/L (1 grain) and 85 mg/L (5 grains), with a neutral pH of 7.0 with an acceptable range between 6.5-7.5 pH and target sodium 10 mg/L. The Tea Association of the USA cites 150 mg/L (ppm) with 17 mg/L (1 grain) to 51 mg/L (3 grains) of hardness for the best results.

Water for coffee heated to 195°-205°F (90.5°–96.1°C) will extract all the intoxicating aromas and sweet, delicious tastes. Cooler water will not allow enough coffee flavor to extract, while water too hot will burn the grounds and produce a flat, bitter brew. Tea types that are less oxidized (white, yellow, green, and oolong) are recommended to steep with cooler water, while tea types that are more oxidized (black, Pu-erh, and tisanes) are suggested to be prepared with hotter water.

For both coffee and tea, extraction or infusion times are determined to control the strength of the beverage—soluble concentration and the extraction—soluble yield. Changing the time or changing the water temperature will affect the quality of the beverage for both aroma and taste.

COFFEE BREWING CONTROL CHART
Brewing Ratio: Grams per Liter

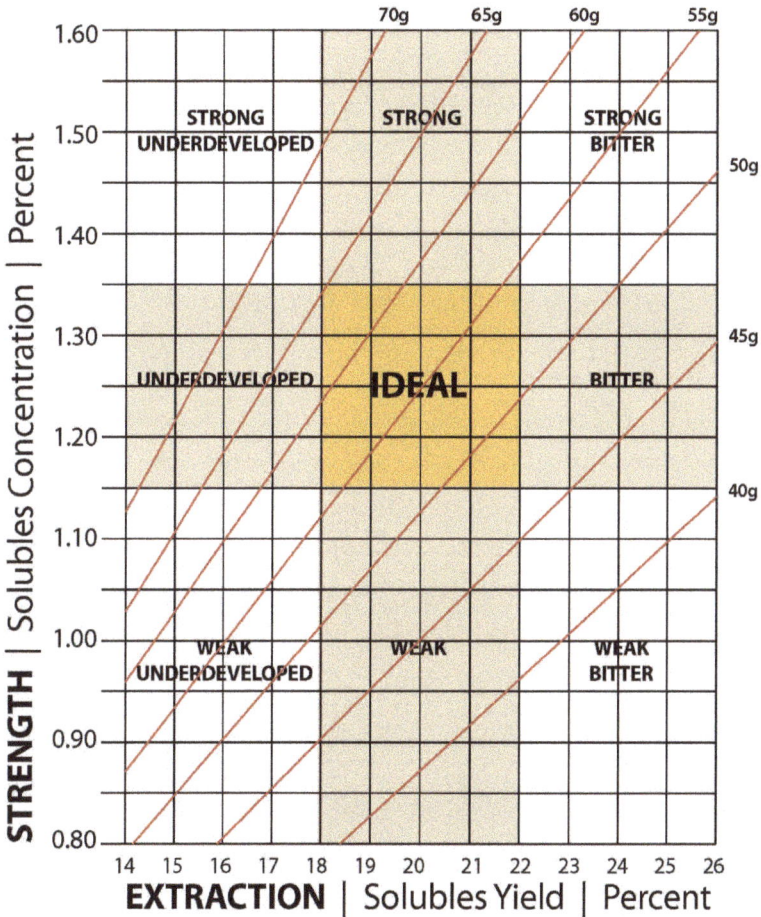

The Coffee Brewing Center, Pub n. 15

Volume is critical in controlling the coffee-to-water ratio and for drip brewers the ratio is 64 ounces of water to between 3.25 – 4.25 ounces of freshly ground fine grind coffee as directed for Gold Cup Standard brewed coffee. The Specialty Coffee Association's coffee-to-water ratio may be expressed as between 1-part coffee to 15 parts water and 1 part coffee to 20 parts water. *(This ratio, water temperature, and water quality will allow extraction of 18% - 22% of the soluble material from the coffee, yielding a brewed coffee concentration (brew solids) at 1.15% – 1.35% soluble concentration).*

5. SERVICE: Brewed coffee is highly perishable; coffee specialists recommend serving coffee immediately after preparation. Holding brewed coffee is not recommended for longer than 30 minutes in glass carafes or 60 minutes in thermally sealed carafes. Extended holding times cause the aromatics to dissipate, reducing sweetness and allowing the acidity to become sour and bitter. During long hold times brew solids continue to cook and water evaporates, which changes the flavor and reduces the quality of the beverage.

Providing training to control the quality of coffee beverages will help protect your company's reputation and build a following of loyal customers. Are your customers drinking delicious coffee beverages prepared using the five key elements for coffee quality?

There are many methods to brew coffee beverages: immersion brewing is steeping ground coffee in hot water (percolation, drip, and French press). Drip brewing uses gravity to draw the hot water through coffee grounds into a separate cup or carafe (automatic machines and manual pour-over units); pressurized brewing uses designed force to push or pull the hot water through the ground coffee (espresso machines, column brewers, and siphon brewers).

Drip is the most popular brewing method for both commercial and consumer beverage preparation. The manual pour-over method requires the person making the coffee to heat the water separately then pour the hot water over the coffee. An automatic machine will heat the water internally and dispense the hot water over the coffee to produce the beverage.

Automatic drip equipment is more popular than manual pour-overs; however, the manual hand-crafted processes are gaining in popularity for both at home and within foodservice and specialty coffee establishments. As a result, the design of automatic coffee-makers has evolved to become more efficient, precise, and easier to use. The new generation of automatic drip equipment may include digital controls for water temperature and water dispensing. Control panels may include brew timers and allow user customizations. Automatic equipment may have safety features for beverage quality to prevent brewing when the water is not at the proper temperature, or to prevent the brew basket or coffee carafe from being removed during the brewing cycle.

Temperature settings on commercial foodservice equipment are used to compensate for high-altitude brewing, or for user-defined customizations.

Hot water dispensers are often used for preparing tea and manual pour-over coffee brewing. Hot water taps dispensing near boiling water have been popular in homes for many years. Most commercial hot water dispensers have default temperature settings at between 201°F (93.8°C) and 205°F (96.1°C). Many commercial units can be customized for user-defined dispensing temperatures. Many coffee brewers have hot water taps to prepare tea beverages or simply for instant hot water on demand. This hot water is typically drawn from the same reservoir of water used to make coffee. Thus, water temperature drawn from the hot water tap of a coffee brewer will be based on the user-defined temperature setting, or the manufacturers default setting. FETCO default temperatures are set at 205°F (96.1°C), while Curtis and BUNN default temperatures are set at 200°F (93.3°C).

Company	Brew Volume	Temp. Range	Factory Set Temp.
FETCO	Single 1 gal to twin 2 gal Single and twin 3 gal 6-24 gal capacity	180-208°F	Tank: 205°F; spray head 195±5
Curtis	72 oz 60 oz 1.5 gal 3 gal/6 gal/10 gal 1 gal/1.5 gal	170-204°F	200°F
BUNN	most BUNN brewers	—	200°F

Example of standard factory set temperature.

Service Best Practices

Coffee, tea, and cocoa beverages are highly perishable and beverage quality will rapidly change after preparation. The time between preparation and service should be counted in minutes, not hours. The ratio between the primary flavor ingredient and water changes as the liquid evaporates, as is evidenced by the steam rising from the beverage. Flavor particles in suspension will fall to the bottom and the sweet, pleasing aromatics will dissipate.

Holding refers to the time and manner in which hot beverages are maintained between brewing and serving. For the flavor and aroma of brewed coffee to remain optimal after brewing, three factors are involved: (1) container attributes, specifically the size, shape, and heat retention qualities; (2) the beverage temperature and temperature loss over time; and (3) beverage hold time. All three factors will affect the quality of the beverage and the acceptability to the consumer.

Common ways of storing brewed coffee are in glass carafes and thermal pots. Typically, glass carafes are open at the top and kept on the burner to keep the coffee hot. Glass carafes for commercial brewers usually have a 64-ounce capacity. They have an open top to facilitate easy pouring, which also allows steam to escape causing evaporation.

Thermal pots typically have sealed lids to prevent evaporation and are insulated to retain the heat. Thermal pots are designed for specific holding locations: to be heated on a burner, electrified with internal heating elements, or left off the heat on the counter. Thermal pots are usually stainless steel, are insulated or double-walled with a vacuum between the walls to reduce conduction and convection heat transfer, thus allowing the beverage to retain heat. Thermal pots are designed to be brewed into directly and can have capacity from 64 ounces to several gallons. Thermal pots may have different names, for example, airpots are a type of thermal pot having a manual user depressed pump at the top to

The airpots pictured in the back row and the thermal carafes
in the front are designed to hold hot coffee at a temperature
range between 175°F (79.4°C) and 185°F (85°C).

push air into the sealed pot and the beverage out of the dispenser.
Large thermal pots may be called urns, which is also the name
commonly used to identify large capacity coffee brewers. Both
are popular home-brewing equipment, with appropriate sizes to
accommodate consumer needs.

Best practices within the industry suggest holding temperatures for hot coffee range between 175°F (79.4°C) and 185°F (85°C)—this is not an arbitrary recommendation. Studies done by the Coffee Brewing Center confirm the importance of a constant holding temperature within this range. Any fluctuation of temperature, both high and low, will affect the beverage quality and flavor.

Glass carafes on brewer burners and electrified thermal pots are designed to keep the coffee at a constant temperature of approximately 185°F (85°C) (as measured from the middle of a beverage in the carafe/pot). Non-electrified thermal pots are designed with adequate insulation to maintain the beverage temperatures for an extended period—often several hours. The length of time it is acceptable to hold hot coffee is determined by the quality decision of the business and the amount of heat loss over time for the particular thermal pots.

Holding coffee will affect the beverage quality for aroma and taste as well as the temperature of the served beverage. Best practices are designed for each carafe or pot's heat retention ability and the size and shape of the vessel to maintain the coffee's volatile aromatics and fragile taste compounds. Because these are multiple variables, there is no single answer for appropriate holding times; the decision is based on the perceived quality of the beverage for aroma, taste, and temperature at a specific time for each glass carafe or thermal pot.

I. The rate at which the aromatic compounds dissipate

As hot coffee is held aromatic compounds dissipate and moisture evaporates in the form of steam. Thus, like soup or stew simmering on the stove for long periods of time, cooking and evaporation change the quality of the product.

Aromatic compounds are chemical structures that have an odor and have boiling points below the boiling point of water. Thus, aromatic compounds turn from a liquid to gas and leave the beverage, changing the intensity and the character of the aroma of the coffee as they dissipate. In a closed container, these aromatic compounds will dissipate slower, and the moisture evaporation will condense and drip back into the beverage. The rate or aromatic loss is determined by the headspace within the carafe or pot. Headspace is the measured space between the top of the liquid and the surrounding vessel walls and lid. The rate or aromatic loss is determined by the available headspace, so matching the vessel capacity to the quantity being held is critical to maintaining coffee quality.

If an enclosed container, the aromatic compounds as gases leave the coffee until the vapor pressure in the container reaches equilibrium, at which point the gases leave and enter the coffee at the same rate.[5] When the headspace is minimized in a sealed container, the gases reach equilibrium quickly, and the aromatics are mostly preserved until coffee is dispensed. As fresh, cooler air enters the headspace from dispensing the hot liquid, the beverage temperature will reduce as well.

II. The rate at which flavor compounds change within the coffee

The brew colloids—oils, insoluble materials, and sediment suspended within the beverage—impart flavor when brewed and the rate at which these taste compounds change is primarily a function of the holding temperature, the manner in which temperature is maintained, and the length of holding time.

Chlorogenic acid (CGA), at approximately 15% of the soluble compounds in brewed coffee, has the most impact on the coffee's taste. When chlorogenic acid breaks down, it breaks down into caffeic and quinic acids. CGA is a primary component of the perceived acidity in coffee beverages along with several prominent organic acids. Caffeic acid is found in many common food items and is commonly described as bitter; quinic acid is found in many plant products and is often described as astringent. The higher the level of these acids, the more sour and bitter the coffee becomes. Therefore, it is desirable and important to hold coffee at temperatures in which chlorogenic acid is most stable because this acid makes up a large amount of the soluble concentration in the finished brew.[5]

Studies done at the Coffee Brewing Center have shown that chlorogenic acid is most stable from 175°-185°F (79.4°-85°C). Applied heat and prolonged exposure to heat (as in the case of a carafe of coffee left on a burner), increases the chemical changes that take place in the beverage. Therefore, thermally insulated pots are best for slowing the breakdown of chlorogenic acid and other compounds in the coffee.

III. The rate at which water evaporates from coffee

Preferred brew strength is not universal for consumers. The Golden Cup Standard from the Specialty Coffee Association establishes an ideal soluble concentration (strength) between 1.15% and 1.45% total dissolved solids in the beverage. The United States ideal is 1.15-1.35%, and the European is 1.2-1.45%.[6] The ratio of coffee to water is critical when brewing, and it is also significant when holding the coffee after brewing. The rate of evaporation is a function of liquid and air temperature and air-exposed surface area.

As water evaporates the concentration of soluble material increases—the coffee becomes stronger and more potent. The breakdown of chlorogenic acid and other soluble materials in combination with the increased concentration of these compounds due to water evaporation creates a highly unpleasant taste.[6] To avoid water evaporation from the coffee while maintaining its temperature at 175°-185°F (79.4°-85°C), it is an industry best practice, as well as our recommendation, to hold coffee in sealed, insulated containers.

Holding time is one of the most variable elements of serving coffee. As with many businesses, foodservice operators experience vacillating periods of customer rushes and lulls. Although these times may have a certain degree of predictability from historical data, it is nevertheless difficult for foodservice operators to predict accurately how much coffee to brew at any given time of day. Even if held at 175°-185°F (79.4°-85°C), the flavor of the coffee will still break down over time. A customer could walk in the door right after the coffee has been brewed or when a pot of coffee has been sitting for an hour or more. Some coffee businesses have set a specific time limit after which they discard the coffee and brew a fresh pot. This practice regulates freshness, and it also means that if not properly planned, a lot of coffee can be wasted.

Each foodservice company will determine the operating specifications based on changes in coffee quality and temperature loss for the equipment. Some companies may hold coffee for as little as 20 minutes after brewing in an open top glass carafe, or as much as 90 minutes or more in a sealed thermal pot.

Traditionally, and relative to hot coffee, fewer Americans are hot tea drinkers, which is why many teas are made to order instead of prepared and kept ready in urns or thermal pots. Additionally, because different teas require different temperatures for brewing, as well as specific infusion times to extract distinctive flavors, it is not yet a widely followed foodservice practice to prepare and keep quantities of tea warm in holding containers. Also, the quality of tea degrades over time and is a factor in many U.S. foodservice operators' decisions to prepare the beverage to order, rather than making and holding the tea in teapots or thermal containers.

For these reasons, hot beverage best practices include brewing coffee throughout the day and preparing tea to order to ensure freshness and optimal quality.

Temperature Loss Tests

Conducted at Coffee Enterprises, spring 2018

Temperature loss over three hours in a thermal airpot of coffee

Brand and Size of coffee maker: Curtis Large
Coffee/Water: 9 oz coffee/1.5 gal water
Brew Time: 6:40 minutes

Time Elapsed	Temperature
0 minutes	183.1°F (83.9°C)
30 minutes	180.3°F (82.4°C)
1 hour	179.0°F (81.7°C)
1.5 hours	178.1°F (81.2°C)
2 hours	177.0°F (80.6°C)
2.5 hours	176.0°F (80.0°C)
3 hours	175.1°F (79.5°C)

Average temperature loss every 30 minutes in airpot = 1.3°F

Temperature loss of steamed milk in a 12 oz. paper cup with simulated sipping

Time Elapsed	Temperature
When it stopped steaming	153.3°F (67.4°C)
1 minute	150.8°F (66.0°C)
2 minutes	149.0°F (65.0°C)
3 minutes	146.7°F (63.7°C)
4 minutes	144.4°F (62.4°C)
5 minutes	142.6°F (61.4°C)
6 minutes	140.9°F (60.5°C)
7 minutes	139.4°F (59.7°C)
8 minutes	137.8°F (58.8°C)
9 minutes	135.6°F (57.6°C)
10 minutes	133.5°F (56.4°C)

Average temperature loss per minute while "sipping" = 2°F

Temperature loss of a single shot of espresso

Time Elapsed	Temperature
Immediately	165.2°F (74°C)
1 minute	154.4°F (68°C)
2 minutes	149.7 °F (65.4°C)
3 minutes	146.0°F (63.3°C)
4 minutes	142.3°F (61.3°C)
5 minutes	139.0°F (59.4°C)

Average temperature loss per minute = 5°F

Single shots of espresso lose approximately 5°F per minute.

Serving Hot Beverages

Many examples of what can go wrong during the transfer of the beverage to the consumer have been presented in preceding chapters. There are inherent risks in any foodservice environment when hot food and beverage products are served. For example, in restaurant dining establishments, servers regularly warn guests to be careful when the plates are hot.

Typically, service for hot foods in foodservice establishments is closely aligned with formal table service where the server places the items directly on the table in front of the guest. This is an example of a foodservice best practice. Informal or casual service where the server hands the items to the waiting hands of the customer is not recommended. This is particularly troublesome or dangerous when food is served in the cooking vessel, such as pizza and fajitas. Serving any hot liquid requires extra attention from the server to prevent spills and potential injury to oneself, the guest, or anyone else in the vicinity. For this reason, servers are very careful to place bowls of soup and stews, etc., directly on the table. They are not passed directly into a customer's hands. Hot beverages also require similar service and care.

This example of best practices for service with guests seated at a table in a foodservice establishment has many critical components:

- the server recognizes and understands the risk of serving hot items and/or items that may spill;
- the server warns the guest of the dangers of hot foods and/ or hot serving vessels;
- the customer recognizes the risk and acknowledges the risk by allowing the server to perform their functions unimpeded.

After product quality, aroma, and taste, the most important aspect of foodservice standards is the transfer of food and beverage items from the kitchen to the server and from the server to the guest. Chefs and restaurant managers will add that presentation

Making a good cup of tea or coffee (or cappuccino) is part art,
part science, and always must be handled with care.

and appearance are of enormous importance. Great care must be taken to maintain the integrity of the food or drink presentation as jostling or tilting cups, plates, and bowls will cause the food or drink items to shift in slipshod arrangement or spill. Furthermore, management will insist on the most efficient conveyance of food and beverage from the production areas to the guests to maintain temperature: hot foods served hot and cold foods served cold. Within the argument that quality is paramount also lies the integral concept that maintaining the health and safety of both server and guest is a well understood rule.

Handling the Cup

The best practice for servers handling cups, glasses, barware, stemware, or any other beverage vessel is to consider the vessel as two sections: the top part for the guest and the lower section for the server. The top half of any drinking cup or glass is reserved for the guest who will place their lips on the rim to sip of drink the beverage. For sanitary reasons, even when servers wash their hands frequently, servers shall avoid handling the cup or glass in places where guests will drink. Servers should always handle cups without handles and glassware from the bottom half.

Cup Transfer

Safe serving of hot food and drinks in restaurants and café settings are familiar procedures and easy to understand; nonetheless, it must be clearly and consistently conveyed that any and all hand-to-hand hot beverage transfers must be avoided due to the serious burn risks if spilled.

Kitchen to server – Best practice for health and safety require the food or beverage item to be placed on the counter or a table to be collected by the server.

Table service – Best practice for server to seated guests shall be for the food or beverage item to be placed directly on the table in front of the guest. Hand-to-hand transfer, even when initiated by the guest, should be avoided.

Best practice for refilling cups to seated guests shall be for the cup to be stationary and set down on a table or counter in a location convenient for the server to reach. Refilling guests' cups that are presented in mid-air shall be refused; cups should be refilled only when stable and placed down on the table or counter.

If a carafe is used for guests' independent table service, the carafe should be placed in the center of the table or directly in front of an adult and out of children's reach. This is to avoid inadvertent spills that may occur if the table is bumped or jostled or there is a clumsy reach.

Counter service – Best practice for server to guests standing at counters shall be for the server to place the cup down on the counter for the guest to pick up independently. When there is no defined service counter area the hot beverage shall be placed on a secure, non-slip tray to allow the guest to remove the cup from the tray independently.

Drive-thru service – Best practice for server to guests at drive-thru windows shall be for the server to place the hot beverages in a purposeful, secure, carrier tray or hot drink caddy to allow the guest to pick up and remove the item independently. Or, if there is a secure service counter extending from the interior of the restaurant at a height and distance convenient for guests seated in vehicles to reach easily and safely, the best practice shall be to place the items on the counter for the guest to pick up independently.

Public or private transportation (airlines, trains, ferries, etc.) – Best practice for server to seated guests on methods of public or private transport shall be for servers to place hot beverages in a purposeful, secure, carrier tray or hot drink caddy to allow the guest to pick up and remove the item independently. Airplanes, buses, trains, ships and ferries should have installed, stabilizing, effective cup holders for travelers use and safety. This is imperative to help prevent spillage from the jostling of hot liquids due to the expected and unexpected movements of fellow travelers and the turbulence of travel in moving vehicles. When no cup-holder exists, the guest shall be made aware of hot beverage spill and burn risks through a verbal warning as well as product warnings on the cup or lid.

In sum, servers should place hot beverage items safely down on tables or counters to be picked up by guests independently and/or hot drinks must be safely conveyed to customers on non-slip trays or in purpose-built and secure hot beverage carriers. Public and private transportation companies have the added responsibility of providing adequate cup-holders for travelers' safety. We contend that these safety protocols should be universal practices for all businesses that serve hot beverages—including quick service and limited service restaurants as well as airlines.

Prepared vs. Deconstructed

Coffee and tea are unique from other beverages because the guest may finish preparing the drink by adding condiments such as sweeteners and dairy products. Soft drinks, cocktails, beer, and wine are all served as a complete final beverage—there are no other flavor alterations to be made by the guest. (Although there certainly may be some exotic beverages other than coffee and tea that do require modification by the guest, for all general purposes, this categorization is accurate.)

There is debate about whether hot beverages should be served to guests fully prepared or should be served "deconstructed" and modified by the guest. For the purpose of best practice recommendations for handling hot drinks safely, the distinction between prepared and deconstructed hot drinks is focused on spill prevention and risk reduction—the safety of the server, purveyor, and guest. In all cases, adding condiments to unlidded hot beverages should not be done while in a moving vehicle and guests shall be given verbal and written warnings at point-of-purchase and service counters.

Prepared beverages are served to guests with all condiments added by the server. Sweeteners and/or whiteners are not provided separately to guests.

> **Drive-thru window service and service on public/private transportation** – Best practice is for servers to fully prepare the beverage for the guest. Providing separately packaged sweeteners or dairy products shall be avoided whenever possible. This is advised due to the compounded spill risk for consumers when adding condiments to hot drinks while in any moving vehicle. Servers should always prepare hot beverages at a stable, non-slip surface.

Deconstructed beverages are served to guests without added condiments. Sweeteners and whiteners are provided separately for guests to add to their beverages.

> **Server to seated guests** – Best practice for restaurants or cafés is to place all condiments on the table for the guest to add independently.

> **Server to standing guests** – Best practice for counter or bar service is to make all condiments available to the guest at a specific counter station or table location away from other busy foot traffic and out of harm's way. Offering single use packages of condiments, such as sweeteners and dairy products, at to-go counters shall be avoided if possible. This effort is to encourage guests to fully prepare and lid beverages before leaving the premises and to discourage the preparation of hot beverages in moving vehicles. Best practice shall be to offer guests all condiments at the counter in tabletop carafes or dispensers whenever possible.

Lids

Coffee and tea to-go are a well-defined market segment, and presently, disposable to-go cups are ubiquitous for serving hot beverages—although there are indications that reusable travel mug usage may be on the rise. Most companies provide disposable cups, lids, and trays to make on-the-go hot beverages efficient for the guest and effective for the foodservice establishment. Some businesses also offer reusable travel mugs for purchase as well. As with other service standards, our recommendations for best practices concentrate on spill prevention and the safety protection of both servers and guests. It is not necessary to lid hot drinks served in restaurants or cafés to seated guests.

Travelers and to-go hot beverages – Best practice requires that all drinks served to travelers and to-go shall be served with secured, locking lids. Unlidded cups of hot beverages should not be served to guests for any to-go orders. This recommendation remains firm whether guests are pedestrians, in vehicles at drive-thrus, or are passengers on any public or private conveyance, such as airplanes, buses, ferries, trains, etc.

Secure locking lids shall be placed on top of the cup by the server (regardless of the materials used for cups) before the beverage is transferred to the table, counter, or carrier tray for the guest to pick up.

When a guest presents a reusable travel mug without a lid and requests to secure the lid themselves, the guest shall be made aware of the spill and burn risks through a verbal warning. The server will also draw the guest's attention to warning signage at the point-of- purchase counter

There are real and tangible risks for drivers and passengers when adding condiments and consuming hot beverages in vehicles. All guests traveling with hot drinks to-go will be encouraged to prepare or to have their hot beverages fully prepared and lidded before entering moving vehicles. Critical risks are obviously attached to drivers with hot drinks in hand: adding condiments, fiddling with lids, and consuming hot drinks while driving distracts from giving full attention to the operation of the vehicle; conversely, focusing on the operation of the vehicle distracts from the process of adding condiments, lidding the cup, and consuming the hot beverage safely. Operating a vehicle demands the driver's full attention and handling a hot beverage does too. Underestimating the dangers associated with driving while handling hot drinks puts the driver at risk, puts passengers at risk, and puts other nearby vehicles, drivers, passengers, and pedestrians at risk too.

Passengers also have an obligation to remain alert and aware of the risks and hazards when traveling with hot beverages. They are also constrained by space, speed, and seatbelts and cannot assume that they will have the flexibility or opportunity to speedily get out of harm's way from a hot beverage spill. Consumer awareness and handling with due caution are necessary too.

Fully prepared and securely lidded hot drinks to-go are necessary for travelers' safety—regardless of whether the server or the guest prepares the drink—it must be done on stationary, stable surfaces while standing on solid ground.

Warnings

Caution, warning, and direction signs have become ubiquitous within foodservice establishments. There are signs and notes to alert employees and consumers of action to take, situations to avoid, and warning to be aware of.

- Actions to take: wash your hands, order here, pick-up here, pay server, etc.

- Situations to avoid: employees only, do not enter, etc.

- Cautions and warnings: consuming shellfish, consuming raw or undercooked meat, tree nuts on premises, calorie content, etc.

Consumers can become familiar with the interiors of foodservice establishments and desensitized to all of the signage. Their primary focus is concentrated on reading the menu to decide what to order, as well as determining how and where to proceed. With so much visual and written information, the consumer may tune out the peripheral information and become blind to what might seem to be of less immediate and compelling concern, such as essential warning signs.

Creating effective warnings that consumers will notice in this environment is akin to developing an effective educational program. Both are multi-step processes that require passive and active communications.

People remember…[7]

10% of what they read
(current state of caution and
warning notes on cups and lids)

20% of what they hear

30% of what they see

50% of what they see and hear

PASSIVE
LEARNING

60% of what they read, hear, and see

70% of what they say and write

90% of what they do

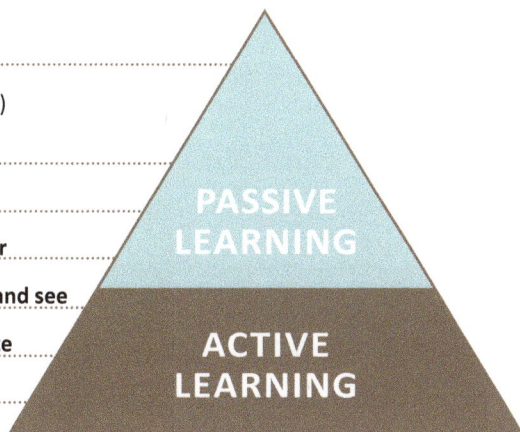

ACTIVE
LEARNING

In terms of raising consumer awareness about the hazards of spilling hot beverages, active learning suggestions are obviously not applicable—writing (i.e., signing waivers) would not be appropriate in foodservice settings, and learning from doing (spilling/burning) is the very hazard we hope to avoid. Therefore, a more reasonable and modest goal in terms of issuing hot beverage hazard warnings would be to try to raise consumer awareness and increase caution by 60 percent.

For these reasons, we recommend a three-step approach to warning communications to prevent injury when handling hot beverages.

Step 1 – Clear warning label on cup and lid

Already embraced by many stakeholders in the beverage industry, however, it needs to be recognized as the minimum reasonable action to warn consumers. ANSI informed and easily recognized icon and warning sign to alert consumers of the danger of handling hot beverages must be created and consistently used on all hot beverage cups and lids. ANSI is the American National Standards Institute.

The warning sign using easily understandable words covers the 10% rate of retention by providing something to read.

The warning icon will cover the 30% rate of retention by providing an image to see.

Step 2 – Verbal warning at hand-off

Required employee training in handling hot beverages safely should be embraced by the restaurant industry and hospitality universities as the minimum reasonable action to guard against the hazard and warn consumers.

A concise verbal warning statement should be given to all consumers when served a hot beverage, such as "Handle with care! Hot beverage spills can cause serious burns." Although this statement may seem inappropriate within a restaurant or café when the guest is seated and served in a cup or mug, it should be considered a required warning whenever hot beverages are served takeaway— at drive-thru windows or when taken from a café to-go counter to drink in a vehicle. Servers should encourage all travelers to have to-go hot drinks fully prepared and lidded before exiting store or entering vehicles.

The verbal warning along with the warning sign and icon on the cup and lid increases the retention rate of the warning to take appropriate action to 60%.

Step 3 – Visible warning posted at point of purchase

Additional warning notice with icons on signage at all points-of-purchase. This is foodservice operators last opportunity to issue a warning before the consumer assumes the greatest risk. Signage should also urge all travelers to have to-go hot drinks fully prepared and lidded before exiting store or entering vehicles.

For example, placement of warning notices could be at the point of beverage transfer in a restaurant drive-thru window, at the pick-up and/or condiment counter of to-go cafés, as well as integrated into the existing warnings given to automobile drivers about the distracting driving hazards of in-dash computers and GPS. Additionally, warnings should be posted on airline and automobile tray tables that suggest avoiding the consumption of hot drinks while vehicles are moving, etc. These efforts serve to reinforce step #1.

Foodservice operators and employees should consider these steps and warnings as the minimum reasonable requirements for standard operating procedures and begin to include these best practices in their operations immediately.

Our overall goal is to educate all servers and consumers of the inherent risks and hazards of hot beverages and to encourage safer handling. Through procuring safety-tested, strong, thermal cups with spill-proof and secure-fitting lids, training employees, and the issuance of three different consumer warnings—written, visual, and verbal—we believe that the hospitality industry will have done what is right and what is within its domain to protect themselves and their customers. And, furnished with their tasty hot drinks and good information, consumers should, in turn, find that a reasonable person assumes responsibility for their actions and heeds the warnings and handles hot beverages with much more care.

Coffee Enterprises
Brewing & Service Best Practices
SUMMARY

1. BREWING AND HOLDING
Coffee Brewing and Holding Temperatures

- **Brewing Temperatures** – Chemical analyses confirm that the 195°F to 205°F range of coffee brew temperature causes the proper extraction rate of chemical compounds from the coffee grounds and makes coffee with optimum flavor profiles.

- **Holding Conditions & Serving Temperatures** – To maintain brewed coffee at optimal flavor and freshness, the coffee industry and Coffee Enterprises recommends holding brewed coffee away from direct heat and in a thermal container at 175°F-185°F. Coffee should be freshly brewed throughout the day with a maximum holding time of 60 minutes.

Espresso, Cappuccino, Café Latté, Tea and other hot beverages

- **Espresso** – Industry best practices for espresso preparation are to use hot water between 190°F-200°F.

- **Café lattés and Cappuccinos** – Industry best practices for steamed milk temperature range of 150°F-160°F, which is well below the 180°F scalding temperature that adversely affects the microfoam texture.[8] Food safety regulations state fresh dairy should be heated to above 140°F.

- **Teas** – Water temperature is specific to each tea category: 160°F for white, yellow, and Japanese green. 175°F for Chinese green, 195°F for oolong, 205°F for black and tisanes. 210°F for Pu-erh.

- **Teas** should be prepared to order to ensure freshness and optimal quality.

2. HOT DRINK PREPARATION

Prepared – All condiments are added to the beverage by the server.

- **Drive-thru window service and service on public/private transportation** – Servers should add all condiments for the customer. Providing sweeteners and dairy products in packets or other packages should be avoided whenever possible.

Deconstructed – All condiments are added to the beverage by the customer.

- **Table service for seated guests** – Condiments are placed on the table for the guest to use.

- **Counter or bar service for standing guests** – Condiments are available for guests at a specific counter station or table location set safely aside from other busy foot traffic areas. Condiments shall be in tabletop carafes or dispensers whenever possible. Warning sign shall be posted at counter station requesting all guests prepare beverages at the counter before leaving.

3. SERVING HOT BEVERAGES

- **Handling the Cup** – Servers should hold all cups by the handle or bottom half of the cup.

- **Cup Transfer** – Hand-to-hand transfer shall be avoided due to the inherent risks of spilling.

  - **Kitchen to server** – Beverage to be placed on the counter or a table to be collected by the server.

  - **Table service to seated guest** – Server to place beverage on the table in front of the guest.

  - **Server to guest (refilling cups)** – The cup to be stationary on a table or counter in a convenient location for the server to reach. Cup presented in the air by the guest for refilling shall be refused and only refilled when stable on the table or counter.

    If a carafe is used for guests' independent table service, the carafe should be placed in the center of the table, out of children's reach, and verbal warning given.

  - **Counter service** – Server to place the cup down on the counter for the guest to pick up independently. When there is no defined service counter area, the hot beverage shall be placed on a secure, non-slip tray to allow the guest to remove the cup from the tray independently.

  - **Drive-thru window service** – Server to place the hot beverages in a purposeful, secure, carrier tray or hot drink caddy to allow the guest to pick up and remove the item independently. Or, if there is a service counter extending from the interior of the restaurant at a height and distance convenient for guests seated in vehicles to reach easily and safely, servers shall place the beverage on the counter for the guest to pick up independently.

- **Public or private transportation (airlines, trains, ferries, etc.)** – Server to seated guests on public or private transportation shall place hot beverages in a purposeful, secure, carrier tray or hot drink caddy to allow the guest to pick up and remove the item independently. Airplanes, buses, trains, ships and ferries should have installed, stabilizing, effective cup holders for travelers use and safety. When no cup holder exists, the guest shall be made aware of the risks through a verbal warning and product warnings on the cup or lid.

4. LIDS

• **To-go and take-away service** – Secure locking lids shall be placed on top of all disposable to-go cups and reusable travel mugs by the server (regardless of the materials used for cups) before the beverage is transferred to the table, counter, or carrier tray for the guest to pick up. Unlidded cups of hot beverages should not be served to guests for any to-go orders.

When a guest presents a reusable travel mug without a lid and requests to secure the lid themselves, the guest shall be made aware of the spill and burn risks through a verbal warning as well as warning signage at the point-of-purchase counter.

• **Public or private transportation** – Airplanes, trains, and other means of public or private conveyance shall serve and require all hot beverages to be in an 8-ounce or smaller cup with a secured, locking lid.

• **Restaurant seated table service** – Hot beverages may be served in an unlidded cup or mug with condiments on the table.

5. WARNINGS

- **Written and visual warning labels on cups and lids** – ANSI guidelines should inform icon and warning designs and alert consumers of the danger of handling hot beverages. Warnings should be prominently displayed and consistently used on all to-go hot beverage cups and lids.

- **Verbal warnings** – A concise warning statement should be given by servers to all consumers when served a hot beverage, such as "Handle with care! Hot beverage spills can cause serious burns." All travelers shall be encouraged to have to-go hot drinks fully prepared and lidded before exiting store or entering vehicles.

- **Point-of-purchase warnings** – Warning notices with ANSI-informed hot beverage hazard warnings shall be displayed on signage at all points-of-purchase. Condiment counters should include warning signage to encourage all hot beverages be fully prepared and lidded before exiting store or entering moving vehicles.

6. EMPLOYEE TRAINING

Best practices for safely handling hot beverages shall be required training for all employees serving hot drinks to the public. Hospitality and other related college programs for restaurateurs and the food and beverage industry shall include hot beverage handling safety in educational training programs. Airlines and other public or private transportation companies that serve hot beverages to guests must also be trained in best practices to handle hot drinks safely and to provide appropriate first aid.

Commercial Operations

After a Spill: Good Samaritan First Aid and Recording the Incident

When hot beverage spills do occur, quick, timely, appropriate, and humanitarian responses are required. Scald burns need immediate first aid and substantial burns also require urgent and professional medical care.

FIRST AID FOR SCALD BURNS

Step 1: Help the injured party.

DO Stop the burning.

Hold the burn area under cool running water or immerse in cool water for at least 10 minutes or more.

For skin areas that cannot be immersed, such as a burned face or genital area, apply clean, cool, wet cloths to the burn area. Be sure to keep cloths cool by adding more water. If the face or eyes are burned, have the person sit up as much as possible, rather than lying down—this helps to reduce swelling.

DO remove any clothing or jewelry that is near, but not stuck to, the burn area.

DO cover the burn. Use dry, sterile dressings or a clean cloth to cover the burn. Apply a loose bandage or drape a layer of cling film over the burn area—a clean plastic bag could also be used for burns on a hand or foot. Covering the burn helps to prevent infection.

DO protect the burn from pressure and friction.

DO keep the person warm but take care not to rub any material against the burn area.

DO calm and reassure the person that you are prepared to help and call emergency first aid responders if needed. Get the contact information of the injured party, if possible. Also, offer to call a family member or friend on the person's behalf for further support.

DO NOT use ice or ice-cold water. This can cause shock from body heat loss.

DO NOT apply ice, ointments/lotions/creams, butter or other fats, medicines, or other household remedy to a burn.

DO NOT remove any clothing or material that is sticking to the burned area as this may cause further injury.

DO NOT breathe, blow, or cough on the burn.

DO NOT disturb blistered or dead skin.

DO NOT give the person anything by mouth if there is a severe burn.

DO NOT place a pillow under the person's head if there is an airway burn. This can close the airways.

When to Contact a Medical Professional

Major burns will need immediate medical attention. Call for trained Emergency Medical Technicians for any of the following instances:

- You aren't sure how serious the burn is
- Skin is red and has blisters
- Swollen, peeling, red, white, brown, or black charred skin
- There is more than one type of burn at a time, or more than one part of the body is burned
- Burn is 2-3 inches wide or larger
- There are second-degree burns on the hands, feet, face, groin, buttocks, genitals, or over a major joint
- A child, frail, or an elderly person has been burned
- Victim is having difficulty breathing

- A person exhibits *any* symptoms of Medical Shock

  Shock symptoms include:
  - Cool, pale, ashen, clammy skin
  - Rapid pulse or breathing
  - Nausea or vomiting
  - Enlarged pupils
  - Weakness or fatigue
  - Dizziness or fainting
  - Changes in mental status or behavior, such as anxiousness or agitation

Step 2: Record the incident

(Example of an incident report form is in the appendix.)

- Fill out an incident report form promptly

- Record the injured party's name, contact information, and a written statement of what happened. Include the time, location, and nature of the accident, as well as any first aid or other offers of assistance given and accepted or refused.

- Recover any products involved in the spill, such as the cup or lid, if possible.

- Take photographs of the incident and/or the location of the incident, the machine involved, and the cup as soon as possible.

- Gather names, contact information, and record written statements from other employees or any customer witnesses

- Give this report to supervisors and managers and keep the report on file.

- Check and record temperatures and settings of all machines involved in the production of the drink as soon as possible following a spill. Have a representative from the machine company or an outside party come and verify temperatures from the machine(s) involved and whether the machines were working correctly.

- Management should follow-up with the injured party and show concern for his or her well-being, although a retailer or legal advisors may have other policies and recommended procedures regarding contact with an injured party after the incident. Keep track of any communication with the injured party. If possible, acquire copies of all emergency responder reports.

- Keep all paperwork records on file.

Step 3. Lawsuit Concerns

If a lawsuit claim is filed after a spill and burn incident, decide whether to settle or contest the claim. Cases involving an employee's hot beverage spill onto a customer usually should be settled. However, hot beverage spills where the plaintiff was solely in charge of the beverage during the spill, should be contested—especially if based on an unjust claim that a beverage made to industry recommendations was unreasonably dangerous or excessively hot. Prepare a strong defense with at least one expert witness who can testify authoritatively on temperatures needed for the preparation of quality of hot beverages. Continued claims about the appropriate temperatures for teas and hot coffee threaten the high-quality standards of the hot beverage industry, are not necessarily based on facts, and do not correctly identify or contribute to solving the real problem at issue: Handling hot beverages safely.

Citations

1. http://www.ncausa.org/Industry-Resources/Market-Research/National-Coffee-Drinking-Trends-Report 2018 - Review

2. http://scaa.org/PDF/resources/golden-cup-standard.pdf

3. American National Standards Institute, ANSI's *Standards Management: A Handbook for Profit* Reprinted by permissionof the National Electrical Manufacturers Association

4. Proceedings of a National Coffee Burn-Spill Seminar, May 21,1999,Chicago, IL. Specialty Coffee Association of America.

5. Ted R. Lingle, *the Coffee Brewing Handbook, A Systematic Guide to Coffee Preparation*, published by Specialty Coffee Association of America, 1996.

6. *Coffee Brewing Workshop Manual, Publication 54.* (New York: Coffee Brewing Center of the Pan-American Coffee Bureau, revised 1974)

7. http://www.basicknowledge101.com/photos/2015/cone_of_learning_web.png

Afterword

I have been asked to consult in many more hot beverage spill and burn lawsuits during the year that this book was nearing completion. Most of the incidents involved drive-thru service operations and included our favorite hot beverages —coffee, tea, and cocoa. The underlying issue was not and is not about the standard brewing temperatures of hot coffee or other hot drinks. It is about handling hot drinks safely so that spills and burns are avoided.

This statement holds up in court. When I have testified in front of juries at civil trials on behalf of defendants, all decisions have been in favor of the defendant. Restaurants (and their insurance carriers) have been willing to defend their practices and operations. And, when they go to trial , they often win—but even so, it costs to be right. The time has come for the industry to act with pragmatic, proactive, and principled implementation of consumer safety initiatives that will mitigate hot beverage spills and burns. If these steps are successful, the lawsuits will fall away. This requires making improvements in cups, lids, carrying trays, serving counters, as well as in educational and employee training programs. It also requires more effective hazard warnings in order to raise consumer awareness about the need to handle hot beverages with greater caution and care.

I know that there are considerable up-front costs in launching such proposals, but I also know that an ounce of prevention is worth a pound of cure. As consumers, we have been willing to pay for product improvements and safety, such as with automobiles, pharmaceuticals, certain food packaging, and machinery. Do most people complain about cars having seatbelts or airbags? That's doubtful. Let the hot beverage industry follow suit and implement safety standards and product improvements for cups, lids, serving trays, warnings, and employee training. The cost of prevention may be balanced with reduced expenses for litigation and insurance premiums. Any new expenses incurred could also be shared with consumers; although this would add to the price of their drinks, more importantly, their skin would be saved, and the pain avoided would be immeasurable.

Within the pages of this book, I've shared the 38-plus years of industry knowledge, experience, and research that inform my opinions. And, I do not stand alone in my point of view. As noted in the Kalsher, Phoenix, Wogalter, and Braun study cited in chapter one, "How do People Attribute Blame for Burns Sustained from Hot Coffee,"[4] the researchers also concluded, "Finally, there is a need for research to systematically investigate how defendants might be viewed if they were to take steps to decrease the likelihood and extent of injury, such as changes to the design of the container (e.g., to the cup and lid), more effective warnings, or better employee training practices ."

We are starting to see the next generation of consumers usher in an era where environmental concerns could eclipse the call for disposable hot beverage cups, and in their place, reusable thermal cups with locking lids become the norm. This would be ideal: better for holding hot liquids safely and better for the environment. We have already begun to see the call to reduce waste in terms of plastic straws and polystyrene cups in New York, Seattle, Miami, and Washington DC. Further down the road, we may also find other safety features become standard, such as vehicles equipped with gyroscopic-leveling cup holders and drive-thru service windows with telescoping and height-adjusting counters. But in the meantime, I'll offer my priorities and reiterate recommendations for the next steps to take to mitigate hot beverage spills and burns:

1. Industry acceptance and adherence to the use of universal hot beverage hazard warning labels and messages on all hot beverage cups

2. Training for all foodservice employees in the safe serving and handling of hot beverages

3. Implement safety testing and industry-wide standards for all to-go hot beverage drink containers

4. Urge restaurants to adhere to the use of cups, lids, and trays that meet or exceed these quality standards

5. Alert airline, train, ferry, and other transportation providers to the hazards of hot beverage spills and encourage operations that protect the safety of passengers and employees: quality cups with secure, spill-proof lids, proper hand-offs, effective cup holders

6. Advocate that retailers with drive-thru windows offer to prepare and lid all to-go hot drinks for customers (to avoid lid removals in cars to add cream or sugar) and when possible, install more accessible counters for servers to set down and customers to pick up hot beverages independently

7. Encourage the hot beverage industry to join forces to raise public awareness about the hazards of hot beverage spills, the possible consequences of such a spill, and the importance of more cautious handling

Consumers have shown, repeatedly, that they do not realize how quickly serious burns can happen with a hot beverage spill. We can deliver our hot drinks with more effective warnings and safety measures now—or we may find ourselves served in court later.

With thanks,
Dan Cox

Acknowledgments

To learn the nuances of making a good cup of coffee has taken almost a lifetime of experience and knowledgeable, supportive colleagues. To gather all the information and insight necessary to make this book has also taken a decade of experience as consultant and expert witness in litigated coffee spill incidents as well as an accomplished assembly of generous friends and colleagues.

I am grateful for the many contributions of my colleague, and Coffee Enterprises' Vice-President, Spencer Turer, for his technical advice and meticulous editorial review, chapter by chapter, as well as his contribution of Chapter 4 Best Practice Recommendations for Commercial Operations. His extensive knowledge and experience in the foodservice industry have made it possible to offer informed and realistic suggestions to assure safe and practical operating policies and procedures.

I am also grateful for the editorial and peer reviews from my esteemed friends: Ted Lingle, former executive director of Specialty Coffee Association of America and author of numerous trade books on coffee and a titan in the field of coffee; Richie Berger, senior counsel at Dinse, Knapp & Erdman and Chuck Door of Door Law provided strong legal background on litigation issues; David Leitner, MD of the University of Vermont Medical Center for oversight in the chapter on scald burns and first aid after a spill.

Thank you to photographer Julia Luckett who brought her visual storytelling talent as well as a consumer's eye to the many images illustrating the technical equipment and varied serving environments of today's quick service to-go coffee.

Thank you to graphic designer Lindsay Francescutti for the cover design and for putting all of the facets together—photos, charts, graphs, and text—to make an eye-catching and cohesive read.

Lastly, editor/mentor, and friend Lin Stone was the glue that kept this book together and moving forward. She was a delight to work with and gentle with her objections and advice, which were needed and appreciated from beginning to end.

May all your coffees be aromatic, flavorful, and safely sipped in good health.

Dan Cox

Appendix

Example Incident Report Form

Your name: _____

Job title: _____

Supervisor: _____

Have you told your supervisor about this incident/injury?   Yes   No

Date of incident/injury: _____   Time of incident/injury: _____

Name of injured person: (please print)

_____

Contact information

    Phone: _____

    Email: _____

    Street Address: _____

_____

Customer's Statement

(Please describe the incident and any injuries in detail):

What happened?

_____

_____

_____

_____

_____

What part of your body was injured? Please be specific.

_____

_____

_____

Customer's signature: _____   Date: _____

Employee Statement

What happened?

_____

_____

_____

_____

_____

What part of the customer's body was injured? Please be specific.

_____

_____

_____

_____

_____

Where did it happen?

_____

_____

_____

_____

How did you respond/offer to help? (First aid? Call EMTs?) Describe.

_____

_____

_____

_____

_____

_____

Employee's Signature: _____ Date: _____

Were there any witnesses to the incident?

Witness #1 contact information (Please print):
Name: _____
Phone: _____
Email: _____

Witness Statement:
Please describe what you saw.

_____
_____
_____
_____
_____

Witness signature: _____ Date: _____

Witness #2 contact information (Please print):
Name: _____
Phone: _____
Email: _____

Witness Statement:
Please describe what you saw.

_____
_____
_____
_____
_____

Witness signature: _____ Date: _____

Contributors

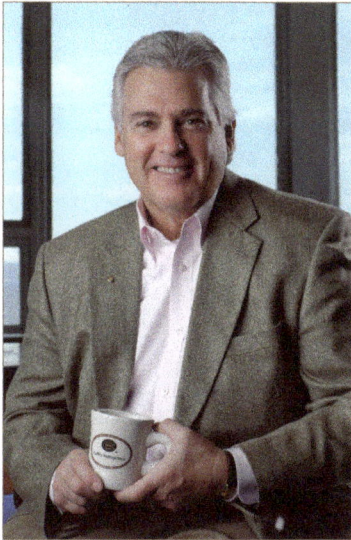

Dan Cox is a leading authority on the Specialty Coffee Industry and brings more than 38 years of practical experience in management, roasting, cupping, product development, and marketing. He is president and owner of Coffee Enterprises. The companies maintain extensive physical and sensorial testing labs and are the largest privately held coffee and tea analytical labs in the US.

Cox has earned industry recognition for his extensive knowledge and lifetime of work: three-term president of the Specialty Coffee Association of American (SCAA) and chairman of both the Coffee Development Group and Coffee Quality Institute. He was honored as the SCAA's "Man of the Year" and later earned the organization's Lifetime Achievement Award.

Cox co-founded Grounds for Health (GFH), a nonprofit organization that brings health care services to more than 100,000 women in five coffee-producing countries. He was also appointed president of the Coffee Kids Advisory committee, a non-profit organization dedicated to helping children of coffee-producing countries.

Cox has traveled to twenty-two coffee producing countries and toured more than 170 coffee roasting facilities worldwide. He has been a guest consultant for the media, including *Good Morning America*, *Good Morning Guatemala*, MSNBC, National Public Radio, CNN, China Global Television Network. He has also written many trade journal articles: *Business Week*, the *Chicago Tribune*, *Seattle Times*, *Boston Herald*, *USA TODAY*, *Eating Well* magazine, among others.

Dan holds a bachelor's degree from Norwich University and was inducted into its Athletic Hall of Fame. He served as a captain in the US Army, volunteered as an emergency medical technician, and was elected a justice of the peace.

Dan continues to offer senior tasting expertise as a licensed Q Grader and is a consultant for strategic management and expert witness in coffee litigation cases involving beverage temperatures.

Julia Luckett is best known for her photojournalistic approach to photography. Whether it be an intimate wedding on the shores of a lake or an international trip to document the lives of coffee farmers, she brings a keen and observant eye to every project. Her work has been featured in *National Geographic*, *British Vogue*, *Roast Magazine*, and other publications.

Spencer Turer is vice-president of Coffee Enterprises and began his coffee career in 1994 as a barista-café manager and first roasted coffee in 1995. Spencer is an active volunteer in the coffee industry, serving the Specialty Coffee Association on the Research Center's Advisory Council and Chairman of the Standards Committee. He is a member of Technical & Regulatory Affairs Committee of the National Coffee Association, a member of the E18.06 Sensory Evaluation: Food & Beverage Committee for the American Society of Testing & Materials, and on the Specialty Coffee Arbitration Panel for the Green Coffee Association. As a founding member of the Roasters Guild (now Coffee Roasters Guild), Spencer served on the first executive council and led the creation of the Roasters Guild Roaster Certification Program.

A respected writer and technical editor, Spencer is a member of the Editorial Advisory Boards for both *ROAST* magazine and *Tea & Coffee Trade Journal*. He is a regular reference source and an industry "insider" for the news media and academic researchers.

Spencer is a graduate of Johnson & Wales University, earning degrees in Culinary Arts and Foodservice Management. He is licensed by the Coffee Quality Institute as a Q Grader. He has earned the SCAA coffee diploma and is a certified lead instructor, Golden Cup technician, and coffee taster. He is also a Roasters Guild Certified Coffee Roaster. Spencer was honored by the Specialty Coffee Association of America with the "Outstanding Contribution to the Association Award" and received the Patron Award for extraordinary volunteer leadership.

www.ingramcontent.com/pod-product-compliance
Lightning Source LLC
Chambersburg PA
CBHW041915190326
41458CB00024B/6274